GPS Millionaire

The Secret of the Ages for the 21st Century

Bruce McGregor
&
Raymond Aaron

Copyright © 2016 by Bruce McGregor & Raymond Aaron

No part of this publication may be reproduced or transmitted in any form, or by electronic or mechanical means, including any information storage or retrieval system, without permission in writing from the publisher.

ISBN: 978-1-77277-089-6

Published by
10-10-10 Publishing
Markham, Ontario
CANADA

Contents

Dedication	v
Foreword	vii
Introduction	ix
Chapter 1: Growth, Prosperity and Success	1
Chapter 2: Great Purposes Support	9
Chapter 3: Giveaway Past Situations	25
Chapter 4: Genius Power Stimulates	45
Chapter 5: Greater Potential Self	61
Chapter 6: Growth Principle – Serenity	69
Chapter 7: Growth Principle – Success	79
Chapter 8: Grander Personal Surprises	89
Chapter 9: Goals Predict Success	99
Chapter 10: Great People Surround	109
Chapter 11: Growth Principle – Gratitude	123
Chapter 12: Grow Potential Self	133
Chapter 13: Growth Principle – Spirituality	143
Chapter 14: Generous Prosperity Sensibililty	157
Chapter 15: Gain Profitable Synergy	169
Chapter 16: Gain or Pain Solutions	185
Chapter 17: Give Profound Service	207
Chapter 18: Genuine Positive Sensitivity	219
About Bruce McGregor	231

Dedication

*This book is dedicated,
with love,
to my amazing wife,*

Gail McGregor

*She is the inspiration
and support for everything
wonderful in my life.*

Foreword

By

Jack Canfield

New York Times bestselling author of
The Success Principles
and co-creator of *Chicken Soup for the Soul*®

In April 2015 I had the opportunity to meet Bruce McGregor, aka The GPS Guy, when I was speaking at Raymond Aaron's *Create Your Own Economy Event* in Toronto, Canada. Since I sometimes mention the idea of the GPS (Global Positioning System) device in my talks with audiences and discuss how important it is to use your own inner guidance system to move towards wealth, it caught my attention that Bruce McGregor had already written a book on the subject – *GPS Wealth: Your Roadmap to Growth, Success and Abundance*. Raymond Aaron and I presented an Achievement Award to Bruce McGregor for his book at that event.

Bruce McGregor & Raymond Aaron

Now Raymond Aaron and Bruce McGregor have written a book together: *GPS Millionaire: The Secret of the Ages for the 21st Century*. This wonderful book combines the classic wisdom of Robert Collier (*The Secret of the Ages*) with the timeless information, updated knowledge and awareness you need to become a **G**rowth, **P**rosperity and **S**uccess (GPS) Millionaire today. Listen and act on the instructions you receive from these pages. There really is no other way. The GPS concept is a great idea whose time has come! The clever use of the GPS letters and this book, GPS Millionaire, offers the opportunity for you to create an incredible life for yourself – a life overflowing with GPS! (**G**rowth, **P**rosperity and **S**uccess).

Introduction

Ideas are not powerful in and of themselves. They have power only when they are acted upon and brought into the world in a real way for others to see, learn about and understand. Using your imagination to create ideas and to take action on those ideas over and over again develops your personal power in a REAL way – not as a hope, dream or wish.

I still remember thinking about the GPS metaphor for the first time. At that moment, the GPS metaphor was the idea I began to develop that compared a GPS device – a Global Positioning System physical device – to a comparable, but biological GPS device or mechanism inside every person. They are similar and comparable in that when you switch on a hand-held GPS device – the first thing it does is show you where you are on its screen map. The second thing it does is ask you where you want to go. The third thing it does is tell you approximately how long it will take you to get to where you are going on the map. When you provide that information input, the GPS device proceeds to devise and then present to you the most efficient and effective way for you to proceed to arrive at your destination along with the timing. Voila! There you are – from where you are to where you have said you want to go!

Additionally, the GPS device provides multiple route options that can slow your time down a little as you choose the route you prefer to travel along the way to your destination. It works absolutely perfectly every time and is available in pretty much every country around the world.

I remember where I was when the idea came to me. I was in Vancouver with my wife, who was attending a conference. I have a cousin who lives in Surrey, B.C., which is a suburb of Vancouver. My cousin, Ron, had invited me to go with him that day to play a round of golf. He is an avid golfer and I am not – but I was on my way to meet up with him, looking forward to a fun day on the course and conversation, since we had not seen each other for a while. I took the SkyTrain, the oldest and one of the longest automated driverless light rapid transit systems in the world – a huge part of Vancouver's rapid transit system – an above ground train that is clean, fast and reliable. En route to Surrey we were suddenly crossing the Fraser River. I had not been on the SkyTrain before, but suddenly, as you cross the Fraser River, the sky and the panoramic vista just opens up on this massive river view in all directions with the glorious Rocky Mountains in the background. It is a breathtaking scene and the crossing lasts for about 5 glorious minutes. It was a beautiful, clear day and the view was spectacular and inspiring!

My wife was attending her conference session that morning and I was travelling alone. About half way through the crossing above the Fraser River, as I was being immersed in the fantastic, natural beauty of this spectacular vista of glorious mountains and glistening water, the GPS idea was born in my mind. Wham!! I thought – this is a fantastic concept that I must develop and explain to others to help them to understand just how easy it is to have great wealth in their lives – in their health, their career, their relationships and in their finances. My first book – ***GPS Wealth – Your Roadmap to Growth, Success and Abundance*** was created at that moment

As I continued to reflect on my GPS metaphor for success, I called my friends to tell them what I was doing. I called my friend and mentor, Bob Proctor, right from the SkyTrain – while I was still on my way to golf in Surrey, BC. to tell him about my new idea because I was SO excited about it. He was gracious and friendly – supportive of my enthusiasm. I wanted him to work with me on my great idea – he said to me "It's your idea! You should take it and run with it." He was right, and I did. When my book came out the following year, Bob Proctor was kind enough to write the Foreword for ***GPS Wealth.*** I will always be grateful to Bob Proctor for being such an inspiration and for providing wonderful guidance through his Coaching Program and the many other great programs of his that I have been fortunate to be a part of.

I worked on my book in the coming months – chapter titles and ideas for discussion in the chapters came into my mind.

Writing a book is such a fantastic thing – not so much for the writing itself, but rather how it changes the way you look at the world and how the process unfolds for you. It is different for every person. For a few months after I had my book title and chapter titles I could not get anything down on paper. I really just didn't know how to begin, since I had never written a book before at that time. So, one of the first things I did was to contact a graphics designer to develop a book cover for me. She gave me several cover options and I consulted with people I trusted to pick the one that I felt would have the best impact to convey my GPS concept. Then, and this was a big thing, I had the cover made into a poster that was much larger than the actual book size. I took copies of the poster and put them all around my house – in the living room, in the kitchen, in my office. Then, when I got up in the morning and would be starting my day I would say to myself: "There's my book! I had better sit down and write it!"

Over the next few months in early 2014 I did that, chapter by chapter, and ***GPS Wealth: Your Roadmap to Growth, Success and Abundance*** was finished! Then I found a printer in Toronto who I wanted to work with and I self-published my book. It was a fantastic experience and I still remember my excitement when the boxes of my completed book arrived on my doorstep. Now, I had to step out and step up to market my new product to the world – to share the ideas and concepts of GPS Wealth with everyone I could.

At one of Bob Proctor *Matrixx* events in May 2014, he was gracious enough to read from my book to his clients. I served as a facilitator at many of Bob's events over the last 5 years. I have a wonderful picture of him reading to the large audience from my book. I was thrilled as I sat and listened to him speak of my work. I had brought 200 copies of my new book with me to that event and I sold them all! Everyone wanted a copy of **GPS Wealth** – so I developed my own website to market the book and my business online. I realized that when you write a book, you are also creating a business. Once you have created a business in today's world, you absolutely must have a business website. You can still go there to check out what I did for my first business website: www.gpsforwealth.com.

The following September, I was invited by my friend, Peggy McColl, a New York Times Bestselling Author and a mentor and friend, to play golf with her husband Denis and to attend a dinner afterwards at a fundraiser organized by her sister, Judy O'Beirn. I was happy to attend, and Denis and I had a great time on the golf course that day. Denis is an awesome golfer and he just missed getting a hole-in-one by a foot on that day. The dinner afterward was very good and it was a fun event – but as we were closing out the evening, dark clouds appeared overhead and thunder and rain developed quickly. It was amazing how the day had transformed from absolutely beautiful, hot and sunny to a massive downpour with thunder and lightning. What was exciting for me at that event was how the creative process worked again through me on that day. It was at that event that two remarkable things happened.

First, I got the idea at that event for this book – the idea of GPS Millionaire popped into my mind….and as I drove to my home afterward, the next miracle in the creative process occurred. All the chapter titles came into my head as I was driving. When I arrived home, I immediately went into my office and wrote down all of the chapter titles to this book! As you will notice, if you didn't previously know, the chapter titles in my first two books include the initials G.P.S... So, after writing them all down I was immediately a bit nervous that I had duplicated one of the chapter titles I had used in my first book. So I got the book out to double-check that night and – guess what? NONE of the chapter titles I created in my mind on my drive home from Judy O'Beirn's event had been duplicated – they were ALL new and different. Thank you, Universe! …..but wait – there's more…

Second, while at the event, I was fortunate to have lunch with Sandy Alemian, an author and hypnotist from Boston, MA who was also attending. Judy O'Beirn introduced me to Sandy. As we were having a lovely conversation through lunch she turned to me and said, "You know, I love the idea of your *GPS Wealth* book, but I think it also stands for something else." "What is that?" I replied. "Growth, Prosperity and Success," she said. WOW!! Thank you, Sandy, Judy and Peggy! (…and the universe, again!!)

My GPS Brand took off in a GREAT new direction on that day!

Several months later, I attended Raymond Aaron's 'Create Your Own Economy' event in the spring of 2015. I had the great pleasure of not only meeting and talking with Raymond Aaron; I also met his guests Jack Canfield and Loral Langmeier. I received an Achievement Award at the event from Raymond Aaron and Jack Canfield for ***GPS Wealth: Your Roadmap to Growth, Success and Abundance***. Jack Canfield mentioned to me that he thought the GPS concept was fantastic and he encouraged me to develop it further. When I contacted Jack Canfield to write the Foreword for this book, he eagerly accepted. Thank you so much, Jack. You are such an inspiring person to me and to millions around the world! Thank you!

I am thrilled and delighted now to be co-authoring this book: ***GPS Millionaire – The Secret of the Ages for the 21st Century*** with my friend and mentor, Raymond Aaron. Raymond is a New York Times Top Ten Bestselling Author and a world-renowned Speaker and Master Teacher. I am SO grateful to have the opportunity to share this material for you with Raymond Aaron. Raymond is a blessing in my life and he will be in yours, too! Thank you, Raymond.

Bruce McGregor & Raymond Aaron

As you will learn in this book, the classic wisdom of Robert Collier has been such a blessing in my life. His ideas and inspiration are the reason for the subtitle of this book. I hope you benefit, as I did, from the GPS thoughts that he shared with the world almost 100 years ago. That wisdom, updated and enhanced for our time, is here to help you right here and right now within these pages.

Take the information provided to you in **GPS Millionaire** – read it, study it, reflect on it and take action on it. It will only help you if you take action on it to improve your life. I know you can do it. These principles are not mine – they are time-tested through the ages and they have delivered massive success over and over again to ALL of those who were wise enough to apply the principles to their lives in a dynamic and active way. Now, it's your turn – you must study, and then DO IT!!!! You're the Best! (YTB!) - To your continuing Growth, Prosperity and Success. I am The GPS Guy!

Bruce McGregor
Toronto, ON
June, 2016

Chapter One

Growth, Prosperity and Success

No one can follow the history of life down through the ages without realizing that the whole purpose of existence is GROWTH--expression. Life is dynamic--not static. It is ever moving forward--not standing still.

Robert Collier

You cannot possibly move forward in your life until you decide that your Growth, Prosperity and Success is the most important thing for you to focus on en route to becoming a millionaire. Nothing will happen in your life that is lasting and fulfilling until you have made this decision. Yes – it is a decision. You must choose to become a GPS Millionaire.

Change is everything. You cannot sit still, or stay in the same place you are today, not even with your current accomplishments and achievements. Life only knows more life. There is always more to go, even when it seems like others are trying to put you down or limit your development. I did not settle for what I was told was possible. As a young man, I did not settle for working on cars or being a high school teacher or a musician. When I reached my goal, I set a new goal and raised the bar. There was more to do.

Why do so many people struggle to earn enough money to live from month-to month? How can most people make so little headway in life that they are constantly finding themselves without the means to really enjoy living? What makes the difference between just getting by and being in a position to seize opportunities as they come along? When will the masses begin to understand that in order to achieve a goal, you must start first by having one – a goal that motivates and excites you to get up every morning and keep moving toward it?

I was not privileged. My family was a lower-middle class working family and this limited our horizons and our view of life. You see, we were taught to believe that there was only so much you could do. Of course, that wasn't true and, as a young person, I didn't buy it. I went out and did what I believed I could do and I succeeded. It surprised me when that happened, so I worked on another goal and I succeeded again. The truth is that I learned that our limits are self-imposed. By working this way on my goals, I managed to erase the barriers put in my own way and replace them with a new way to move forward – the GPS way. If I can do it, so can you.

The world now, early in the 21st Century can be a mysterious and mystifying place – most people in large urban areas are rushing around in a frenzy of activity, trying to earn a living, struggling to make ends meet with not enough month at the end of the money. Technology, we have been told, will simplify and streamline our lives – but is that truly the case? Certainly we can see some tremendous benefits, but is life busier or slower than it was five or ten years ago? The human condition deceives us into believing the 'group speak' of experts who tell us constantly on the news what their perception is, what they believe our perception should be and what they believe is the truth for us. Is it the truth? In most cases, I think not.

The key is finding your center. It is not limiting yourself in any way or letting others limit you. Decide to be open and broad-minded – make sure that the road you choose ALWAYS focuses on your personal growth. Only in this way can you imagine prosperity and take action to gain success – the success you deserve.

You must choose to follow your own GPS road to the million dollar destination you seek. Without this decision, you will wallow in the swamp, doing no more than keeping the flies off and going nowhere. Nothing lasting and fulfilling will ever come to you without making the decision to move forward, to move on, and to get in a better direction – a GPS Direction!

More hurried, rushed and frenzied activity does NOT lead you to your GPS Millionaire. It goes in the other direction! It leads, over time, to disease and disaster for your body – and it clearly indicates that you are NOT in control of the way you are living your life. Take a moment right now and look around you – What are you listening to? What influences are you allowing to persuade you to behave in this mindless frenzy? How is it affecting your daily living, your relationships with friends and loved ones, your career process? Are you moving forward or are you moving backward?

The GPS Millionaire method that I am giving you is the first step. It worked for me. It can work for you. I don't want to keep this knowledge to myself. I want to keep growing, so I am sharing this information about success in life to teach you how you can grow, too. I am teaching you my GPS Millionaire method so you can be the best you can be. Your tremendous success will continue to grow and further our success as we work together. I want you to achieve outstanding and amazing success!

I am teaching you to tap your unique potential and reach for incredible results. You will feel better about yourself and you will gain more self-confidence to set new goals. You will prosper and, as you prosper, you will gain more success. Each success leads to the next success. In five years, you will look back at how far you have progressed, and wonder why you didn't start sooner.

Sometimes it seems like all the days run together in a cycle of bland – you even feel like you are going in circles! You must realize that YOU have the keys to the kingdom here in your hands right now – with this book. If you study this material and take action on it in your life, everything will change for the better for you. It will help you to discover the Secret of the Ages for the 21st Century while you learn to activate, connect with and take action on the guidance you receive from your higher self – your inner GPS!

Do you remember the first time you saw a GPS – a Global Positioning System? …and how exciting it was to learn that you could turn the device on and it would inform you exactly where you were in the world. As you fed instructions into it about where you wanted to go, you would almost immediately learn what steps you needed to take next along a number of potential routes to get you where you wanted to go – to your desired goal, to your destination. You did NOT have to feel lost in the world ever again while you had that device in your hands. What a great feeling of freedom! Who thought of creating this incredible device? You knew then and you know now that a GPS device solves ALL your problems for navigating almost anywhere around the world.

Take a look briefly at how the depressive person lives. People who are depressed see no way out of their mire. They are overwhelmed and they can't see any reason to dream. There is no reason to work for betterment – no reason to get up in the morning. This is a gloomy existence rapidly going nowhere – that is NOT YOU!!

Any goal you choose must motivate you. Your goal must excite you. You must be passionate about achieving it. If not, there is no reason to get up in the morning, no reason to continue through the day--and beyond. There is no reason to dream unless you set goals that will see your dreams turn into realities. That is the GPS Millionaire method – read, study, keep learning, take action and make it happen!

Wouldn't you like to have that kind of GPS device INSIDE you? Where you could access it 24/7 to help you navigate life's hurdles and obstacles on your way to a wealthy, GPS Millionaire life? Now consider this for a moment. The fact is, the technology for the GPS described above has existed inside you for centuries – this is the Secret of the Ages! That's right. Why do you think that 1% of the population controls over 95% of all the money that is being earned in the world today – right now? Do you think this is an accident? It is NOT an accident – the wealthiest 1% in the world have been using their inner GPS for Wealth for centuries. Now it is your turn to apply this information in your life and become a GPS Millionaire!

If you see yourself as prosperous, you will be. If you see yourself as continually hard up, that is exactly what you will be.
Robert Collier

Chapter Two

Great Purposes Support

The mind in you is the mind that animated all the great heroes of the past, all the great inventors, all the great artists, statesmen, leaders, business people. What they have done is a small fraction of what still remains to do--of what people in your day and your children's day will do. You can have a part of it. Stored away within you is every power that any man or woman possessed. It awaits only your call.
Robert Collier

All of us are hard-wired to achieve success. Each of us is born with a unique set of differing amazing talents, skills and abilities that sets us apart from each other, but also joins us in a common mission. I believe that we were put on this earth for a reason – that reason is to grow and develop our talents, skills and abilities to the furthest extent possible throughout our lives. Applying ourselves on a daily basis to be excellent people – to make the best effort we can to make the most of those talents and abilities in order to improve not only our own lives, but the lives of our families and those we touch or come in contact with

– always aspiring to live an excellent life, a life of Growth, Prosperity and Success.

Heroes are not born – they develop through life. Then, they make a decision to act. Some heroes are reluctant to be heroes. But they are put in the position of having to make up their minds to do something …or not. Act or die. Act when the time is right and when action is called for or be a nobody and do nothing. This is the same question Hamlet faces in his "to be or not to be" soliloquy.

Inventors are not born, either. They develop through trial and error and their own response to failure. Their road begins with ideas and excitement. Excitement begets motivation, a desire to create and apply that knowledge. Inventors make a decision to act. Edison is perhaps the best known example of an inventor. People learned later that he had failed 10,000 times in his efforts before creating the first electric light bulb. Edison saw it differently. He said: "I have not failed. I have just found 10,000 ways that won't work."

We are all born with a particular talent – a unique strength that we enjoy and are passionate about. But no matter how talented you are, talent will only take you so far. After that, you must work. You must apply your talent in a way that maximizes what you can offer to others. Always do your best – decide to work and do whatever it takes. Make a decision and make up your mind that this is what you are going to do.

I knew a very talented young musician. She had an easy, natural voice. Her talent carried her through four years of college. She was given, because of her natural ability, the opportunity for a full scholarship to a conservatory. She lost the opportunity because she did not work to take her beyond that moment of success. She produced a recital that was easy, requiring little or no effort on her part. Later, she was offered another opportunity, an opportunity that would have set her up for life. She did not take it. She did not want to work. Sometimes the fear of our own success is greater than our fear of failure. Often we take the easy way out and do not challenge ourselves to do our best, no matter what! Today, she teaches children piano in a small, unknown town, earning enough to make it month to month. She never took advantage of the opportunity to challenge herself to see what was possible. She decided to settle for being a stay-at-home piano teacher.

All she had to do was make up her mind to work. All she needed was to have a definite goal and to dream big and act on that. To challenge herself to be the best that she was capable of being. Instead, she settled for a life that is less than what she wanted. Just as she was, we are all responsible for the choices we make in life – they define us. They either lift us up to greater heights using our inner GPS, or they leave us settling for a life that is not what was expected – and then the circumstances take control of our lives instead of the other way around. Are you letting your circumstances control your life?

Atul Gawande, MD, in his book *Consequences*, says that the best, most skillful surgeons are the doctors who are willing to work and apply their skills, knowledge and talents. Not necessarily the smartest or the most talented. It is doctors who will do things over and over and over until they are "the best" that are wanted and loved by their communities. This is also how athletes become professionally skillful, stars of the games that they play.

This talent is your tithe of life, your 10% – what you must give back for your success. Ten percent is only a beginning. You must keep on giving and develop your talent through hard work and application.

You have talent? To become great at whatever it is you do, you must make up your mind to work for it. Although the GPS method will set you on your way to a new way of living, you must work to make that promise of success, a reality in your life by being grateful for what you have to share and by giving what you can to help others. This is the only way to be true to your talent and to connect with your inner GPS in a way that helps you to do your best and to move forward towards what you want. This is how you achieve BIG dreams!

Where does this mindset come from?

You are born with it inside.

As you grow, your mind grows and expands. The mind, of itself, never stops its activity. Its job is to find meaning, to figure out the whats and the whys – the hows will take care of themselves. The mind plans and dreams and creates ideas. You don't just dream while you are asleep – your subconscious mind is always working on your behalf 24 hours per day, seven days a week. These waking dreams are the "I want" and "I want to" that directs your life. They are the goals you are pursuing – if you are willing to work for it. You must continue to seek growth throughout your life to achieve your dreams.

You must make up your mind, make a decision and lead it forward. And then you must, like an athlete or a musician or a surgeon, practice and practice and practice. Practice is doing. It is action. This dedication to working is vital. Practice does not make perfect! It makes for success in your life – over and over again. The reverse is also true – if you practice, practice, practice bad habits – failure and misery will be the result for you.

I believe, because of our mind, that we are hard-wired for success. There it is! Why not learn to use it properly? We are not taught this in school – so it is up to us to learn more about our own minds than we have ever known before. Self-awareness is the key to greatness for all of us.

We are here on this Earth for a reason. That reason is to grow and develop our talents and skills. We do this by our mind's making itself up to follow a dream or an idea. The mind is you. The dream is you. Why would you not choose to develop to your fullest extent?

To do this, you must reach out for your own happiness and fulfillment and seek to develop to your maximum ability: this is the GPS Millionaire method that I am offering you. Learning to connect with your Higher Self, your inner GPS – your unlimited potential to achieve Growth, Prosperity, and Success.

You must start by thinking about what you want – what you REALLY want! Let me begin by asking you a few questions and giving you some easy directions to follow. Take a sheet of paper and a pen and write down these questions and make some notes to help you think about these questions. Take a moment and do this now.

What is your purpose?

This is, of course, growth. You are here to grow. But it is much more. It is your individual meaning to life. Where is this idea for you? Why are you here on this planet? What do you really want? Take some time and really look inside yourself for the answer. How do you want to live your life? What are you passionate about doing with your life? Is your life heading towards the goals that you would love to achieve at this time? If not, what has to change for you to move your life in a better direction?

Look inside for the answer.

No one ever found a direction, a purpose, a meaning from looking outside himself. The truth is that you can only control yourself! Everything else on the outside of you is beyond your control. So MANY people do not realize this truth. They spend their lives trying desperately to control other people and things – and then lots more time trying to figure out why that doesn't work. You must look inside. It is more than an isolated intellectual decision. The choice to look inside creates a deeper feeling of yourself, the feeling of your rhythm and your center. Who you are is not outside you. It is not somewhere else. It is in you. Find it. Feel it. You will begin to see your purpose and if you do not see it and feel it DEEPLY on an emotional level – it is not your purpose.

A friend of mine during a life crisis sat down away from the rush and noise of the world in order to feel his inner being. He went past the mirror that others, that society, or your family holds up to us as our identity and he found his purpose. His calling, he told me. He was a teacher. He became an excellent teacher. After his retirement, he continued teaching, for there is more than one road on which to teach others and life is not just about your job or working career.

Discover your purpose, don't make it up.

You cannot make your purpose up. This cannot be faked – it MUST be real to you or you will not succeed. It is that simple. You will not be able to adapt or adopt a purpose that you do not feel completely passionate about. You will not be able to meet the obstacles and hurdles to success that must be faced and overcome them. If your purpose is not true, it is a fake. Why would you want to be false to yourself? You must take 100% responsibility for your life and seek to DISCOVER your purpose by looking deeply inside and honoring what emerges and by making a commitment and a decision to act on what you have discovered.

What is your unique purpose? What separates you from all others?

There is always a special, just-for-you facet to your overall purpose. It is something that is unique for you and no one else. You are unique. It is something you resonate with on many different levels. It is your truth. It is this discovery that connects you with your Higher Self, your inner GPS – your inner spiritual guide to Growth, Prosperity and Success!

Don't reinvent the wheel. Look to the wisdom of the ages for help.

There is no need to spend hours and hours creating a new way of finding your purpose. There have been many, many people who have gone before you who have achieved outstanding results through discovering their purpose. You can stand on their shoulders – and by standing on their shoulders you are able to see farther than if you were just standing on the ground. Many years ago, Sir Isaac Newton was asked in a letter why he was the greatest and smartest man of his generation IN THE WORLD. Sir Isaac replied "It is not that I have been smarter or greater than other men, I have merely stood on the shoulders of the giants who came before me to advance my learning and to improve conditions in the world." Do not disregard all who have come before you. Just because they and their findings are old does not mean they are without worth or merit. Pay attention – keep reading, studying and learning. Seek out the Secret of the Ages for the 21st Century – it is here on the pages of this book!!

Who do you admire?

This should be a person you think most highly of. It can be someone you see as a hero in the world. It can be someone from myth and legend. It can be someone from literature. It can be someone from film or theatre or politics. It could be a person who overcomes many challenges and problems and has achieved greatly in spite of them.

Name the five greatest people you admire who are not in your family.

Why do you admire them?

Do they demonstrate calmness in the face of adversity? Is it their ability to think on their feet? Do they possess the ability to make firm decisions on the spur of the moment? Do they handle adversarial situations effectively, not allowing them to interfere with their personal life?

Find the reason why you admire them. It could be more than one thing. Find it and hold it close to you.

What qualities do/did they possess that you would like to grow in yourself?

You find yourself faced with a question, a challenge, a conundrum? Ask yourself – What would he or she do in this situation? How would they handle this and face it effectively?

What inspires you?

Make a list of 5-10 things that inspire you. What gets you enthused and motivated to do your best? What causes you to pause and say – Wow! – that is really worthwhile and that is something I believe in, too! Then let that great, positive energy flow inside of you and watch what happens as you begin to want to inspire others.

What provides the "juice" for your passion?

What is it that drives you onward? What keeps you going? What gives you energy when you should feel tired and causes time to fly by – so that when you look at the clock, you find yourself saying: "Where did the time go?" If you took this activity away, you'd feel like a deflated balloon.

*Dream lofty dreams, and as you dream, so shall you become.
Your vision is the promise of what you shall one day be:
your ideal is the prophecy of what you shall at last unveil.*

James Allen

Why haven't you achieved your purpose yet?

What is holding you back?

How would the world look if you were 'on track' to your GPS?

When do you intend to get started? (Why not right now!!)

Are you moving closer to your purpose today or farther away from it?

This is the clincher question. For if all the other elements are in place, you will have moved onward and upward. You will feel that you are 'in the flow' heading in the right direction towards your dreams. If you are prevaricating, you will have gotten nowhere. If you have made up a purpose, manufactured one "because someone told you to do this," you will not have made any progress toward your GPS Goals.

There is a thinking stuff from which all things are made of and which, in its original state, permeates, penetrates, and fills the interspaces of the universe. A thought on this substance produces the thing that is imagined by the thought. Man can form things in his thought and, by impressing his thought upon the formless substance, can cause the thing he thinks about to be created.

Wallace D. Wattles

Thoughts? What are thoughts? You can't see them. You can't feel them. In this materialistic, mechanical world you cannot find them. Many people believe wrongly that if you can't see it or touch it, it doesn't exist. Thoughts have no physical body. And yet it is these thoughts that shape our world, drive our mental engines to grow and prosper. It is these thoughts that change the world. Both in worldly terms--ideologies—and in personal terms: what do you believe, what is your purpose, what do you want?

Where do these thoughts come from? They come from the mind – your mind. The mind, too, cannot be felt or seen, yet it runs our lives. You cannot access your mind fully by concentrating and getting lost in the things of the world. This is the kind of thinking that causes addictions and negative habitual patterns that we see around us everywhere in human behavior – they can lead to dissatisfaction, depression and disease. What you want to do is seek out thoughts that are positive and uplifting, that lead you to be inspired, creative and in excellent health. Focus on your great dreams and lofty goals.

You must go inside to really begin to understand what motivates and inspires you. How many philosophies of the world and across all cultures speak of knowing yourself of what you are and what drives you?

Where is the energy you need to move forward?

Why is 'getting lots of money' not a purpose? (i.e., winning the lottery, gaining an unexpected inheritance, etc.)

How can being grateful for what you have serve as a starting point?

What do you need to develop a winner's attitude?

How will your life change for the better when you are living your life purpose?

Improved support, self-confidence, more happiness, enthusiasm and excitement about your life – where is it and how do you find it?

Commit to developing your GPS Millionaire.

Here is the beginning, the outline to travelling on the road to success. Getting your thoughts organized in a new way to move you forward on a daily basis toward your goals. Living a life of achievement – making it happen. How you apply these questions and their answers is the subject of the next chapter.

You can do anything that you think you can. This knowledge is literally the gift of the Gods, for through it you can solve every human problem. It should make of you an incurable optimist. It is the open door.

Robert Collier

Chapter Three

Giveaway Past Situations

It would seem to come back to the old fable of the three blind men and the elephant. To the one who caught hold of his leg, the elephant was like a tree. To the one who felt his side, the elephant was like a wall. To the one who seized his tail, the elephant was like a rope. The world is to each of us the world of his individual perceptions.

Robert Collier

Have you ever wondered what is holding you back in life? What is it that's getting in your way?

You are getting in your way. This is called your old baggage. Past negative experiences are getting in your way. You are carrying them along, often without even realizing it – you are carrying them along with you because they are comfortable, they are part of "the way it is" for you.

Is it? Is this old baggage really "the way it is?" Much of it comes from your childhood. If your father was a rigid, domineering authority figure, you might just have a negative, even antagonizing attitude towards all authority figures. You find yourself stymied at every step. Or maybe you are always in trouble or fighting with others.

Early in your lustful romantic life, your boyfriend cheated on you. You have grown up expecting this kind of behavior from men. You are always suspicious, questioning everything your man does. You set yourself up for yet another failure. All men are jerks. You treat them that way. You fail at relationships or you drive men away. What is this? Old baggage.

This is in both cases, emotional baggage. Each encounter you have adds to this old bag of tricks until it becomes a burden. Heavy, clumsy, you can't get anywhere. You are the one holding yourself back…and deep inside, you know it.

Worse, others know this. They can see you coming and their baggage goes into play: "Uh-oh. Here comes trouble."

Let me give you an example of what happens:

Bobby decides one day, right out of the blue, that he is going to go on a trip. Where? He wants to get away from it all. (A sign of old baggage?) How about Someday Isle? That's an island paradise in the middle of nowhere. That would mean flying but, what the hey! So he packs and goes to the airport. There Bobby finds that no matter what airline he looks at, he has to pay additional charges for his baggage, based on weight and bulk. "That's expensive!" he says to himself. Why? Because we don't like saying things like this out loud – it is more old baggage, in this case about money!

He decides on the least expensive airline. As he approaches the counter, his baggage –his packed emotional baggage that he is carrying around with him that he had got from past experiences, from his family, from his relationships, from his failures – all of this emotional baggage becomes visible to everyone. There is lots of it. And it is heavy! Everyone can see it. How embarrassing!

What if Bobby, and everyone else, has to check all of his baggage, whether physical or emotional, before being cleared for flight? All of that emotional baggage is now costing him a fortune to get on the flight. Not only because it is heavy but because everyone can see it. Wouldn't this be terrible? And everyone shies away from him because they don't want to be associated with him. They don't even want to sit next to him. They are all checking their tickets as Bobby gets his seat assignment, praying they are not his seat mate.

If you had to pay for the load of old baggage you carry around, perhaps you and many, many other people would be unable to go anywhere because the cost of the weight of that baggage would be prohibitive.

Emotional baggage, though, is a human problem. Everyone has old baggage. How can you manage to live if you keep gaining and storing old baggage? We humans are the only animals that carry the weight of our past everywhere with us. Not only this, but we are constantly *adding* to our emotional baggage as every day passes. It grows exponentially because it is played out again and again. This burden can become so great sometimes that you cannot function. But you will not let it go. Maybe you aren't even aware that you CAN let it go.

In one way or another, this is somehow linked to PTSD. Soldiers are not the only ones to suffer. Battered children, battered women, oppressed children and repressed adults suffer too; any kind of traumatic event can become insurmountable old baggage. Once you were bitten by a dog – this becomes a near hysterical fear of dogs because all dogs bite. *All* dogs, even service animals, cause great fear in you. This is an example of the irrational fear that can be created by the emotional baggage you are carrying with you.

This is insane, right? Isn't the definition of insanity--or neuroticism--doing the same thing over and over hoping that one day the outcome will be different? But it can't, can it? You can't get past your old baggage.

This is a recipe for disaster and loss! Just look at all the letters of angst to advice columnists. Look at the problems that psychologists and psychiatrists speak of. Look at the advice-style blogs that litter the Internet.

The problem is that everyone has baggage and they let that baggage come to define them. "I don't know who I am without this." "This is the way I am." and "I don't know what to do about it."

Even though we all have baggage, some of it is good, happy baggage reminding us of pleasant times. But much of it is pretty lousy. So much racy stuff and garbage that we can't find anything good or even remember that there might be good stuff in amongst all the crap.

What's triggering the PTSD every time you want to get something? That's the key point. It isn't that you have this old baggage. It's that you let the old baggage define you. You let the old baggage run your life. So, if you want a life, if you want success, the baggage has to go. You need to let it go. If you can part with your old baggage of negativity, it no longer haunts you. You are free.

Are you a person carrying a lot of emotional baggage?

Why would you ever choose to live this way?

Perhaps a better, more direct and appropriate question is why do you live this way?

How has a lack of thinking about it put you in the wrong place with your emotional baggage? Pinpoint it. See it. See its negative consequences in your life. Learn from that. You are the one responsible for changing this – and you can do it because you are skilled, confident and capable. Because that is the way to a pain-free life, a pain-free world for you. I know that you can do it.

The only way to get to this point is to know yourself. As I noted in the prior chapter, you must go into your personal closet in your mind and discover who you are and what you truly feel before you can begin to make any changes.

Then you can Giveaway Past Situations and reclaim and re-purpose your life. The beginning is letting go of the past without guilt or fear for their loss. You did your best at the time. It is what it is. It didn't work out the way you wanted. Now let it go. You can then move on with your life. You can enable your full potential and unique ability to emerge and come forward. You can soar.

If we regard the fulfillment of our purpose as being contingent upon any circumstance, past, present, or future, we are not making use of first cause. We have descended to the level of secondary causation, which is the region of doubts, fears and limitations.
Thomas Troward

Most people tend to worry about what they are going to do when they are under pressure in the situation of the moment. This contributes to your negative emotional old baggage. You find yourself fretting over how you handled things in the past and keep reviewing them endlessly in your mind: I should have done this, I should have done that. ...then it would have turned out okay. On and on it goes, never ending. You are letting your old baggage run your life it you go no further than this. The challenge is to recognize your errors so that when the next moment of conflict arises you can respond instead of blindly reacting. Then and only then have you made the choice for a better outcome. Then and only then do you have control over your own life.

Between the stimulus and the response there is a space. In that space is our power to choose our response. In our response lies our growth and our freedom.

Viktor E. Frankl

When you are successful, how do you feel? It's a relief! You feel wonderful! Can we do this again?

Oh, yes. We can.

Give yourself the widest range of options by following these simple rules of engagement.

1. Acknowledge reality
2. Release the past
3. Go with something different
4. Guide your focus

Acknowledging Reality

Start by facing straight ahead. Confront reality: this is the hallmark of the world's exceptionally successful people. Take 100% responsibility for your situation. It is not good or bad, it just is. You are choosing how to set a more positive direction with your inner GPS.

Taking 100% responsibility does not mean you are responsible for everything that goes wrong, or for the choices other people make. 100% responsibility also resides in how you deal with difficult and challenging people. Avoidance is not always the best strategy. Old baggage would tell you to succumb and let them run your life, if by no other means than *reacting* to them, accepting their view of the world and not giving yourself a chance to respond to them. If you are not sure of yourself, if you are filled with doubts and fears, you behave with your old emotional baggage, and you already know that does not work.

How can you get to the point that you acknowledge how you should behave differently?

First, write a list of the thoughts, beliefs and behaviors that weigh you down in this situation. Take 10-15 minutes to do this. Don't judge what comes up, just note it down.

Then, reflect on each item and identify whether what you are thinking is really true. They may have been true at one time in the past – but are they true NOW? What would you like the outcome to be now? Visualize it. See yourself doing what needs to be done and having a successful outcome with that person. Acknowledge the painful memories but do not wallow in them. Let them go and focus on seeing yourself successfully dealing confidently with this difficult and challenging person. A new outcome, a much better outcome for you!

Pledge yourself to fostering change and thereby counteract your negative thoughts, the thoughts that do not allow you to see reality. And turn them into affirmations of intent: "I will speak gently" or "I will treat people kindly" or "I will honor myself by responding and NOT reacting." This puts emphasis on future behavior. Positive behavior frees you from the past. You can make these affirmations tangible by reminding yourself of them, much as people do learning a second language: leave a message on the phone, on the refrigerator door, have your cellphone give you a reminder. You are capable, you are confident, you can put your best foot forward, letting go of the past and focusing on a better right now!

Be patient and mindful. Pay attention. Let things play out until the way of choice becomes clear. Because it takes time to make these changes in yourself. You will need less and less the reminders noted above. Every time you feel yourself reacting with old baggage, stop and note this and then let go, gently, but firmly let go. You will only have now what you want.

Release the Past

Get into the habit of setting aside inflexible attitudes. Old patterns of behavior can create inflexibility, and things don't work out the way you want or you experience resistance. At this point, engage in activities that calm your mind. Take the time to stop and see in your mind – the beautiful places in your life, the times when you were most relaxed and happy – fantasize to these moments. Stay there for a time. Enjoy yourself and be happy. Focus on feeling good and feeling grateful.

When you emerge from this exercise you will see the problems, the setbacks, the bad experiences with people in a different light and you will be able to choose what to do without anxiety or fear. Do this every time you run into your emotional baggage. Do this enough and you will find that you can do it more easily and your success rate will increase.

Releasing the negativity of the past allows you to transform the painful and hurtful experiences of the past and go forward into the future in a more confident and positive way. You don't forget what happened; you choose to let them go. Let them sit where they ought to, detached from your emotions, in a place that allows you to be better. It is by learning that we transcend and transform our lives.

Go with Something Different

So, what you are doing is pausing to assess the situation and your reaction to it. That moment of pause is a gift that you give yourself. It allows you to focus on yourself and how you are seeing yourself. Then you can choose to act differently. Ask yourself questions. What is unique about me in this situation? What is unique about this person/these people? What is the challenge here? What is the opportunity for me?

Do you have all the answers? Of course not – no one does and you should never expect ALL the answers to anything. To think you should have all the answers is to get lost rummaging around your old battered emotional suitcase from the past. Acknowledge the reality that you don't have all the answers and, more importantly, that it's not important to have all the answers. If you allow yourself to live in the present moment – you will find all the answers you need as the situation unfolds.

By being patient and letting things happen rather than forcing them to occur as of old, the answers you come up with might just be better and even brilliant for you. They will be different, that's for sure.

A writer friend of mine explained to me the nature of the creative mind when it is simmering along about a story. All of those questions of how the story ends, where it begins, what he's trying to say – they are all bubbling and seeking for attention. But the artist does nothing. He is living on a knife edge, the sharp edge, and he just keeps going along this edge without making any decision. Suddenly an element gets introduced into the process and he falls off the edge into the reality of the story and he can begin writing. He waited and waited for all of the "information" to be in place before he made a decision.

How long does this creative process take? Days? Months? It took Mark Twain seven years to write *A Connecticut Yankee in King Arthur's Court.* It took Thomas Mann 12 years to complete *The Magic Mountain.* Mary Wollstonecraft Shelly took two years to finish *Frankenstein.* But it took Jack Kerouac only three weeks to write *On The Road.* The creative process is unique and works uniquely in every person.

When you allow your mind to follow what's happening without imposing your ego, when you are aware of your old baggage and can let it go, you give yourself a tremendous boost in your strength and power. No longer are you weak – or indecisive. What you are doing, like the writer who lives on the knife edge until "the right moment," is buying time for yourself.

Guide Your Focus

One way to do this is to turn your realizations into a puzzle that needs a solution. This gives you something to solve, it makes you feel empowered. It is also putting the essence of your mind to work. That essence is finding meaning and discovering the whys in a creative way. You get here via knowing your old baggage weaknesses, letting them go and being patient and kind with yourself.

Another way, very much a part of the puzzle approach, is to share your realizations about the situation and your approach. Sharing, talking about it with someone you trust, allows you to work things out. It's that old adage, two heads are better than one. Your mastermind partner will give you another facet, another angle of looking at things with a different perspective.

Now, you are much more powerful. Why? You've got more than one road to travel. You've cleared your own mind and gotten a better focus on what you are doing and what needs doing.

Another way to approach finding a solution for problems is to use a technique called brainstorming. Brainstorming requires you to open your mind and have fun thinking of any solution to the puzzle and writing it down. You need an open mind, like that of a child who's asked how many different ways you can play with an empty tin can or a favorite toy. It is important NOT to judge or assess the nature of each solution presented in the brainstorming – this keeps the ideas flowing until a long list has been generated. If there is more than one person engaging in this puzzle-solving, the results are that much more broad and creative.

To begin with, some of the ideas you come up with may sound outrageous. Remember, though, that you're having fun stretching your imagination. When the brainstorming session is over, then you look over the many options you've come up with and evaluate their possibilities. At this point, you might find something untoward, some approach that is new and inspiring. Because you didn't prejudice your thought process beforehand, you have effectively gone beyond your old baggage, opening up a window of opportunity.

And now you have not just focus but a new focus. Are you strong enough to follow through? Are you committed? If not, you may need to look at your own thinking and take the 100% challenge!

Take the 100% Challenge

Through this self-analysis tool, it is most important to understand your thought patterns. Take my 100% challenge to see if this is so. Assume that all of the thoughts you have during the day totals to 100%, and then begin to categorize your day into thought percentages. Give them a number that makes sense to you!

For example: what percentage of the day do you spend thinking of the past? Past situations, circumstances, events from your life.

Then look at what percentage of your day is spent thinking about the future: where you are going, when will you get there, what your new job will be like; my life will be better when. ...while you are hearing someone speak, are you thinking of what you must do next, what you'll watch on TV, etc.?

Next examine how much of your thoughts during the day are spent on your Task List, the things you feel you have to do. What is that percentage of your daily thoughts?

Finally, calculate as a percentage how much of your day you spent thinking and being in the present moment. The right here and right now. Fully present and thinking only of now.

Although I am not able to predict the exact percentage for you on this last point, on being in the here and now, I will bet that this will be the smallest percentage of all. Your smallest number of the day's thoughts.

Why is this? Why will you spend less time thinking of the now than of the past or the future? A large number of factors come into play.

First, we are not aware of our thought patterns and how we create our preferences to begin with. You will find through this assessment that, perhaps, you are overly focused on the past. Sometimes without conscious awareness, you will choose to spend the bulk of your time living in the past. After all, the past is how you got to be here and now. This is a disastrous choice, however. You cannot be creative in your life when you are simply reliving the past every day of your life.

This 100% Challenge exercise can reveal amazing information to you about you that you had never considered previously. Why are you living with these numbers as they are? While I don't know your numbers, I can predict with *100% certainty* that you need to *increase* the amount of time you are spending in the *present moment*.

The Present Moment is your Point of Power. It is the time when you have the most control to decide and choose where you want your life to go next. However, most people allow the present moment to happen with no thinking attached to it and with no knowledge or awareness of its power. They are living their lives on autopilot. They are asleep in the Present Moment – because they are not there. I assure you that with this type of thinking your inner GPS is set on crashing and burning on a rocky shore.

You need to learn to be present in order to give yourself more choices to proceed toward what it is you want to achieve. You will also give yourself the ability to respond more quickly and in a better manner, rather than to just react to situations as they come up. Life never goes as planned, so better that you are equipped with the tools and, as it were, the inner software to make sure that you give yourself the best chance for great success. Otherwise, you will just, by default, use your old paradigm, your old baggage, and the same cycle will repeat itself over and over as you plod through life. ...as it always has been for you.

How do you get to this point? How did *I* get to this point? "How" questions of this sort are interesting but not really so very important. Most likely, you probably did and do what your parents, teachers and mentors told you or asked you, believing blindly that this would put you on a surefire path to success. This method may have even resulted in a pretty good life for you. But is it the *best* it could be? Is it *your* best?

Are you living, inside, the life that you feel you are truly capable of living? Maybe there is some feeling of things not being quite right. Are you always doing your best or are you doing just enough to get by? You know that you are capable of so much more! Your thought patterns have evolved to where they are now without much conscious awareness on your part. Can you imagine how much further along you would be if you'd been mindful, aware of what it was you were doing "right at this minute"? In the now?

I am sure that you have *never* thought of looking at the percentages of your daily thought processes. Why would you *ever* think that by continuing to do the same things you are doing now that you can ever become more successful, that you can become wealthy?

Becoming wealthy in your life is simply *not* going to happen that way. It will not happen until you do the work required in your self-assessment, not simply to examine your thought processes but to study them in depth so that you know them inside out, so that you know where they came from and what effect they are having on you now and what you will reap in the future as a result of your thoughts. As Henry Ford said, "If you always do what you've always done, you will always get what you've always got!"

But, even then, there will *only* be change when you have actually made the decision to change your daily thought patterns to connect with Source. This puts you in a position to learn and grow as a GPS Millionaire. Then and only then will the changes in your life take you in the direction for not only Wealth and Abundance but for Growth, Prosperity and Success!

In every adversity there lies the seed of an equivalent advantage. In every defeat is a lesson showing you how to win the victory next time.
                                                                                    Robert Collier

Chapter Four

Genius Power Stimulates

The secret of power lies in understanding the infinite resources of your own mind. When you begin to realize that the power to do anything, to be anything, to have anything, is within yourself, then and then only will you take your proper place in the world.

Robert Collier

As you continue and become your GPS Millionaire, to be the best you can possibly be, you must understand this: you must use the power within yourself. You must step up and step out. You must project your ideas and creativity into the world. There is no other way to reach for the stars. You must take action and go for it.

This feeling lies inside you, in that secret closet you are aware of, to discover just what it is you want and how to best proceed to move toward that. As we saw in the prior chapter, you can only accomplish this by getting rid of your old baggage, relegating it to a place now behind your self – in the past. To do this you must step outside your comfort zone and get out of the box. My friend Bob Proctor says that most people have trouble getting 'out of the box' because the instructions on how to do that are printed on the OUTSIDE of the box! I like that idea – there is a ring of truth to it for sure.

This idea can also be frightening to begin with: you've never gone there before; you've never been there before! You are not sure what that is going to feel like for you! Do you have the courage to try something different, even outré for you? Yes. You do. I know you can do it. It is right there inside you, like kindling waiting for your match to fire and ignite a passion that is ready to burst into flames.

My friend Dr. Gay Hendricks calls this zone beyond or outside your comfort zone "Your zone of genius!"

"Really? Surely you jest," you are saying or thinking. Old baggage? Old baggage, your feeling of comfort, says to you – don't do anything out of the ordinary, or something that would make you feel uncomfortable. Be comfortable. Stay in your comfort zone. Sit on the sofa and watch the world go by, like a TV show, and judge it, comment on it, react to it. The truth is reaction is not doing, it is not taking action. You must be *pro-*active and respond, not re-active and out of control.

So you're saying, "I'm not a genius. Edison was a genius, Einstein was a genius, Galileo was a genius, da Vinci was a genius, and Nicola Tesla was a genius. Not me!" As Atul Gawande mentioned, what about people such as first-rate surgeons who keep applying their passion by stepping into their zone of genius to create amazing innovations, like Dr. Denton Cooley or Dr. Michael DeBakey, who came up with brilliant new ways to help and serve others? They weren't born geniuses.

It doesn't matter what obstacles you face in life if you are willing and able to explore this zone of genius in yourself. Walt Disney or Michael Jordan or Will Smith or John F. Kennedy or Michael Phelps or Terry Bradshaw--they all suffered/suffer from ADHD. Let's remember that Alexander Graham Bell was deaf. Helen Keller was blind and deaf. Harriet Tubman and Ray Charles were blind. Stevie Wonder is blind. The "genius" artists who suffered with depression, manic-depression or schizophrenia are legion. Every kind of obstacle imaginable can be used in one of two ways – as a means to prevent you from moving forward with your genius, or as a springboard to help you launch your genius to amazing and new GPS heights!

So, why not you?

I have a friend with a Ph.D. who maintains that getting a doctorate is not a matter of good grades, not beforehand and not during. It is a matter of perseverance. He was not born brilliant or a genius. He was born with talent. But as we've already discovered, talent will only get you so far. Talent will only take you so far; you must work and apply your talent with passion and persistence.

What is "genius?" Well, let's see...to most people it probably represents a person of exceptional intellectual or creative power or other natural ability; or someone very clever and innovative. Often we exclude ourselves as we consider what a genius is – that couldn't possibly be me. So there is a debate both inside and outside as to what a genius is. However, most people can and do recognize it in others far more quickly and easily than they do in themselves.

Thomas Edison said, "Genius is one percent inspiration and 99 percent perspiration." This leads to many other questions – Where does extraordinary talent end and genius begin? To what extent is genius innate or inborn versus cultivated or developed? The deeper we look at and think about genius, the more we wonder – How can we foster it in ourselves and others?

Why is it that we look first for *all* of the reasons we are different or less than someone who has accomplished much? This kind of reaction stops you from getting anywhere. It stops you dead in your tracks! What if you changed your perspective on genius and began to see that within you lies the seed of genius waiting for you to grow it? You know, the SAME genius potential resides within you that was in every one of the people mentioned above!

Well, the reason you've not thought this way is that *you dismissed it immediately* upon hearing of it. You dismissed it out of hand. You dismissed yourself based on your idea of what genius is and who has it. As you can see, your idea, the common belief most people have of genius, is a flawed belief that has not truly been considered. You didn't even think! And you have never truly thought about it.

Would now be a good time to think about your genius potential?

What unique elements do you have that make you different from others? What is *your* talent? What have you worked hard at? What do you love doing? What amazing results would you like to achieve? You already have the proof – if ANYONE in the history of this world up to today has achieved amazing results, despite handicaps, obstacles and challenges – YOU CAN DO IT TOO!!!

Inequality, you shout! Well, a farmer knows much, much more than you do about farming – so, he's better than you. A carpenter knows more than you do about carpentry – so he's better than you, too. Your mother knows more about all that's required to maintain a home than you do – so she's better than you. They're all better than you. This may be what you have been telling yourself through the years! This is false, though. The truth is – No one is better than you. You are NO BETTER than anyone else, but no one is better than you!! Write that down – so you can remember it when those negative feelings of inferiority try to strike at you. Remember it.

What *is* it you do? What is it that you *can* do?

The first step is to reflect and consider deeply what you love and what you do well. I think you will find, upon reflection, that there is a direct correlation between these two – usually you do something very well because you love doing it, so, you do it over and over. This all begins on the emotional level. There are some scientists and philosophers who believe that all decisions are, first, emotional. Reason is only a post-decision rationalization of the emotional reality. Think about it. If you don't like someone's thinking, no matter how rational, you will not believe it, no matter what. Why? It *feels* wrong. You care about it deeply on an emotional level. It is that emotional love and caring that brings a profound respect to doing that thing that you do so very well, perhaps better than anyone else you know.

Do you believe in the Big Bang Theory of the beginning of the Universe? Steven Hawking has discarded this idea. There are some younger astrophysicists who question this theory. If you've ever thought about it, you will have gotten to the point of wondering what came *before* the Big Bang. It had to be made of something! It is only a theory, a rationalization of all the knowledge we have at present to "the beginning" of it all. It is emotionally satisfying to have an answer to it all. That's the mind's job – to find answers.

These scientists are all emotionally involved in their belief. They feel it. They care about it. They work at the astrophysics. It's all so very satisfying to them. This kind of love and caring brings about a profound respect, first for yourself, then for what you do in the world.

But getting to this point is not so easy. For, all along the road, there are those who pooh-pooh your ideas and call you unrealistic and what you are doing just a waste of time. The old baggage begins here, in our youth when we are at a point where our parents and teachers or other well-meaning adults make those negative comments. At that stage, they are probably the only authorities we know. We unquestioningly believe what they say. In many respects, these people are nay-sayers. They may be well-meaning but they are inhibitors, like resistors in a long electric current, or a governor, a device that inhibits performance on motors to limit speed and power.

These nay-sayers, who try to restrain your endeavors and the sharing of your ideas, can have a tremendously negative effect on your growth and on the full realization of your potential if you believe them. Those negative comments are emotionally, psychologically devastating. "You can't do that!" is a massive STOP sign, coming from a respected source. You can become emotionally and passionately stunted and repressed – especially when it is said about something that you are truly passionate about.

Why do we listen to these people? Why do we believe those who speak to us in this negative way? Perhaps they are respected family members so we think they must be right somehow because they are older and more experienced. Could it be that inside us we are awaiting external validation of our passions, feelings, and/or talents? When the validation you seek is not received you stop acting or feeling that way. You shut yourself up. You shut yourself in. You shut yourself off from your own talent! – Unbelievable, but true!!

People who want to be writers but hear their teacher shouting at them, "You can't do that!" never become writers. Surely you know someone who was told you can't do that that then went out and did it, proving the nay-sayers wrong! Why not you?

Quite a few years ago, a young man was accepted into the advanced music program at the University of Toronto's Faculty of Music. The young man came to believe, from others, that the purpose of the program was to produce only concert pianists. Such high level artists performed with orchestras around the world. The young man came to believe he could never play piano at such a high degree of perfection and chose to specialize in a different musical area because of what these people were saying. He was not a very good pianist: that was the truth he gleaned from the message, "If you play, you must play as well as Ashkenazy or Claudio Arrau."

For most of his life, he believed his piano skills were not so good because he believed what he'd been told in his 20's. Yet, whenever he did play in public, people invariably congratulated him on his beautiful playing. All and sundry said they wished they could play as well as he did. It took him 40 years to realize that he was a much better pianist than he had convinced himself he was. Now, he gives concerts – solo concerts – for the community that are well-attended. He receives outstanding reviews.

It might have taken him awhile but he allowed his Genius Power to stimulate him to create the kind of pianist he really wanted to be. He is enjoying his later life immensely sharing his musical talents with others. His creativity has soared. All because he finally overcame a belief that was *false!*

> *Wealth is ultimately nothing more than a subconscious conviction on the part of the individual.*
> *You will not become a millionaire by saying,*
> *"I am a millionaire, I am a millionaire."*
> *You will grow into a wealth consciousness by building into your mentality the idea of wealth and abundance.*
>
> Dr. Joseph Murphy

What do you believe about your inner genius? Are you positive? Are you negative? Are false hopes holding you back from achieving tremendous success in your life *right now?* Or are you one of those people who hear "You can't do that" and goes right out to prove that, "Oh yes I can!"?

It's not so important where or how you got your negative assessment of yourself. You may even understand just where and how they took over your mind. But that's not important. What's important is removing them from your mind. You must overwrite them with positive nurturing and "I can do it" expectations of yourself. It is only in this way that you can move forward and realize your potential.

Don't beat yourself up, or get down on yourself because you probably didn't even realize that this was happening to you. It is what it is. Just do your best to let it go and focus on moving your life forward. Blame and guilt are useless emotions and they only hold you back. Remember – you have always tried your best. No one gets up in the morning from a good night's sleep and says, "Ok – I'm ready now to head out and screw up everything I do today!" No one does that – people go out on their day trying to do their best. They may not have the best plan and they can be sidetracked by not having the best thoughts and energies inside – but they honestly do not intentionally plan to screw up everything in their lives when the day starts. When you were young, hopefully your parents tried to do their best, too! They didn't always get it right, but they tried to do their best with what they knew and had available to them at the time.

This is like the idea of Karma as something that you have that makes your life what it is and there is no escape. You have a bad marriage? That's your bad Karma. This keeps you stuck right where you are. You cannot grow; the original character of Karma is change. You're not stuck with anything. It takes realization, looking and seeing what you were doing, what you are doing. It takes the will to change from deep within to grow, like the upsurge of pressure in a hot spring before it spurts up from the ground and into the air.

The bad Karma, the ill-got idea of what you are (not) is something someone else gave you. Someone else's uninvited judgment of you. You shouldn't feel guilty about this. You've always done your best, given what you knew. You are blameless. But now it is time to set this limiting assessment of your gifts aside and burst into the future. And, if you don't succeed, you learn. People who try to do everything right from the get-go never learn anything. They believe they are perfect and invincible. They never gain the ability to deal with or overcome mistakes and become better. They will inevitably fail at something in their lives. Everyone does.

Luckily you're not like this. But you also don't get up in the morning and say, "Oh. Today I think I'm going to go out and screw everything up. It's a good day to fail." No one does that! You always go out trying to do your best. You may not have the best plan in the world and you may get sidetracked by not having good thoughts and you may not have much positive energy, but you honestly believe you are doing your best. Because that is all you know.

When you were young, your parents and other family members were doing their best to raise you right. They didn't always get it right but they tried and they learned from their mistakes as they lived their lives.

> *Thoughts mixed with definiteness of purpose, persistence and a burning desire are powerful things.*
> Napoleon Hill

Now that you understand about how you are held back, how do you start walking toward your genius potential?

You make a commitment to use your inner GPS and let it lead you forward in the direction of brilliance. You must stop hiding your gifts, your talents from the outside world--and from yourself.

I'm not talking about Ego here. This is not about your Ego. This going after your inner genius is not an Ego thing. This is about allowing yourself to soar. This is about giving yourself permission to let your mind expand and explore what you have and what you can do. And it is about sharing that gift with the world.

It is time for the movement of your mind. It is time to pass on the learning you have and "getting out of the closet" of your mind. There will be, you may be sure, resistance to your new behavior. Some people will criticize you and condemn you for being 'out of the box' – they probably will say you are crazy. Tell you what you're doing is not practical. Impress upon you what a waste of time this breaking out and exploring is. Well, okay. What do they know? More to the point, what do they know about you? *They* are stuck in their own box.

To face this upsurge of negativity, you must commit yourself to making the changes in the first place. You must commit yourself to continuing no matter what. You are moving beyond the mundane and ordinary, just be prepared that others may attack you and demean you and try to limit you. This is their problem – not yours.

My friend, Trace Haskins, the Internet marketing genius, has told me: "I love this quote by Steve Martin and this is what everyone needs to do: 'Be So Awesome that They Can't Ignore You!' " Make your mark – be a wild a crazy guy like Steve Martin!!

The lesson? Do whatever it takes to let your Genius Power Stimulate you--and serve others. When you do this, your life will change dramatically for the better. You will have tapped into your GPS Millionaire and you will have found the secret of the ages for the 21st century for the rest of your life!

But this is only the beginning. For more detailed insights on attaining your goal, read the next chapter.

Our subconscious minds have no sense of humor, play no jokes and cannot tell the difference between reality and an imagined thought or image. What we continually think about eventually will manifest in our lives.

Robert Collier

Chapter Five

Greater Potential Self

Everything is an effect of mind. Your thought forces, concentrated upon anything, will bring that thing into manifestation. Therefore, concentrate them only upon good things, only upon those conditions you wish to see manifested.
Think health, power, abundance and happiness. . . You must realize that, when you have done your best, you can confidently lean back and leave the outcome to Universal Mind.

Robert Collier

How do you escape the sea of sameness and reach for your Greater Potential Self? You must stop worrying about the world of circumstances and conditions and look inside for answers about what it is you truly want. What goal would you like to achieve? What direction do you wish to go to follow your passion and be of service to others? When you begin to consider these questions, you begin to understand how you can move forward in your life.

When I was teaching in Canada, I made the decision that I was going to become a High School Principal. "So what?" you might say. You might also say, "I had a High School Principal when I was in school and he was a jerk!" If that is your reality, my decision may be difficult to understand. However, do you know anyone else who is a High School Principal in the public education system? That one jerk of a principal you knew is not all principals. Do you know how difficult it is to become a High School Principal? Do you know that it is, in fact, extremely difficult to become a High School Principal?

Here is a reality check for you as to why I chose to do this those many years ago. I chose to pursue a path that would offer me the opportunity to become a leader in the public education system in Canada. It was a decision I chose with a lot of care, determination, commitment and, in the end, required a substantial amount of time and perseverance. I did not do this on a whim. I did not do this just so I could be better than anyone else. I did this because my goal was to better myself!

You see, you must look closely at the process that is required to achieve your goal, and then you must look at the results you will have achieved. You must begin by being present in the here and now and develop a vision for your own future. You might say, "Yes, yes. I know what he or she does. He or she is a doctor." You are implying that you know all that is required to become a doctor--and everything a doctor goes through. You imply you know all about his/her training and his/her experiences along the way and his/her everyday work.

Where did you get this knowledge? People tend to believe they "know" certain things – when really, from an experience point of view, they don't. They have no knowledge of the long hours, the loss of sleep, the time away from family, the hard work doing the same thing over and over, the setbacks and the challenges. Do you really know? There is so much information available on the Internet that people believe they "know" certain things. But, in fact, from an experiential point of view they don't know at all. They *think* they know. They *believe* that they know, for sure. But, really, they don't. And then, there is a great deal of wrong information on the Internet.

Every day, then, becomes an opportunity to go back to class, to begin re-learning what you think you know and benefit from learning about it in a new way. That's it. That's the answer.

Let me explain how I came to my decision to become a High School Principal. In the province of Ontario, Canada, where I was teaching, there are, 124,000 teachers in the public education system, both in elementary and secondary schools. Out of those 124,000 teachers, only 2,047 are High School Administrators Principals or Vice-Principals. Vice-Principals don't always become Principals. Of the High School Administrators, there are 915 Principals in the province of Ontario. This means that of ALL of the teachers in Ontario, Canada who *could have* become High School Principals, less than 1% of them actually achieved that position (0.74%, to be precise). There are 115 High School Principals in the Toronto District School Board of Education. Out of 124,000 teachers in Ontario, that represents less than 0.1% of the total number of teachers who became High School Principals in Toronto, Canada (0.093%).

Now, I was fortunate enough to be teaching in Canada's largest school board the Toronto District School Board of Education. The Toronto school district is the fourth largest school board in North America. So, becoming a High School Principal in the TDSB is very prestigious. And it is not easy.

What I am trying to say is that with no assurances, no guarantees, or no "sure thing" and without a solid foundation of support, I made a commitment to become a High School Principal in the fourth largest school system in North America. I believed I could do it. I had faith in my commitment and abilities. I persisted in my belief. And in the end, I became a High School Principal about 5-6 years after I made the decision to go for it.

There were some amazing occurrences along the way. I became Vice-Principal in a school on the same street my mother and her family had grown up on 60 years before. I discovered, while there, that half of my mother's brothers and sisters (my aunts and uncles) had attended the school where I was Vice-Principal. For me, this was a huge confirmation from the universe that my goal was the right one.

At the same time, there were hurdles to be jumped. I recall sitting in my office one day at that school and the phone ringing on December 6, 2000. The voice asked, "Is this Bruce McGregor?" Yes, I replied. "Do you have a brother who lives out in Western Canada?" Again, yes. "This is the Ontario College of Teachers calling. Do you have a brother named Edward Norman McGregor living in Manitoba?" Yes. "Are you sitting down? Your brother died of a massive heart attack in a Winnipeg Hospital on November 27, 2000."

I had been dreading this day. My wife and I had often discussed my brother Ted's possible death somewhere far away and that we would probably be notified by the police. My brother, older by eight years, was brilliant but he was a troubled man. He dedicated his life to education in the Native communities in Western Canada for close to 25 years. He had left Ontario following the breakdown of his first marriage, moving out west to escape the trauma and pain. Though we saw him infrequently after that, our meetings were always good. As he got older, he was fighting diabetes and heart disease. I learned later that he was still fighting his prior demons and had become an alcoholic; he was depressed, still. I attended the Native Memorial service for him when I went out west to settle his affairs. I learned of the love and admiration the Native community had for him. Their love and caring for him was palpable. They felt he was one of them. He made a huge difference in their lives. They all came to give testimony that day about him, some from hundreds of miles away. Ted was only 56 years old.

Life often leads us down roads that are sometimes unexpected and often enough unwanted or unchosen. However, it is up to us to realize that the universe brings us these issues in a way that is BEST for our life. These are chances to reassess ourselves and what it is we are doing. For instance, I had a cousin I was always a bit jealous of. His parents were with him throughout much of his life, until the early 2000's. My parents passed away quite some time ago: my father in 1979 and my mother in 1992. And then my brother died, as noted, in 2000. I was rather jealous that he still had all of his first family alive in his life!

Then, shortly after his parents' 60th anniversary in 2002, his mother passed away. Within a few months, his father passed away. And within 2-3 months his older brother died of a massive heart attack. He was suddenly an orphan. He was the only one left in the family and had to deal with these stunning deaths on his own. Suddenly, my jealousy dissolved. I was sad and taken aback that he had been whacked by such a massive loss and all within the same year! With all of my grieving, I at least was able to spread it out over a number of years in my family.

Life is not easy. Life is difficult. But it is through our higher self that we must live to support and give the best of ourselves to others and to the world. Now, my cousin and I are like brothers because of the challenges we have both faced together in our lives. I am grateful and blessed to have this kind of relationship with him. I love him dearly.

My career path in public education was a long and challenging commitment that involved many obstacles--and much learning. I learned a lot about myself and this changed me. I am not bragging when I say I achieved my goal despite all. After my time as a Vice-Principal, I was appointed to a High School Principalship in Toronto. I worked in that position for many years. I enjoyed and loved working with the students and their parents and the teachers, inspiring them, motivating them. I left my career in public education after nearly 35 years at the top of my game. I was in the top 0.1% of High School Principals.

If you are ever in Toronto, you can go to Lawrence Park Collegiate Institute where I retired as Principal and you will see my portrait picture on the wall along with all of the other Principals who have served since that school was built in 1936. Okay. You're right. That is my ego talking. But that's okay. I'm proud of what I accomplished.

I am here to tell you that you, too, can achieve your goal you can achieve ANY goal you set your mind to. And I want to help you to learn and understand just what you have to do to get there. I want to help you go for it. All you have to do is look inside your Greater Potential Self and follow your inner GPS! You can do it. I know you can. I know you can because I did it.

Plant the seed of desire in your mind and it forms a nucleus with power to attract to itself everything needed for its fulfillment.

Robert Collier

Chapter Six

Growth Principle – Serenity

Ignorance of the power of the subconscious mind is the sole reason for all the failures in this world.

Robert Collier

Do you have peace of mind? A key component of the GPS Millionaire program is peace of mind. You cannot have true success in ANY area of your life without peace of mind or serenity in your life. A person who has this quality radiates calmness and confidence to others. People are inspired by these qualities, though they cannot quite put their finger on it or identify why it inspires them so much. People do not see the connection between the peace of mind and calmness in the person they admire and their own state of mind.

Do you know what peace of mind is, what it looks like for you?

Well, let's think for a moment and take a look at what it *doesn't* look like.

If you travel down the streets of any major city in North America these days, you will have a lot of trouble finding serenity. You will find hundreds, if not thousands, of people rushing around trying to get somewhere using a tremendous amount of energy and showing great anxiety navigating the streets of the city. Many, many people are nervous, anxious, troubled, in pain, not focused, wired up, drugged or liquored up, hustling, competing, striving, angry, frustrated over-stimulated--you get the idea. Frantic, non-stop urban living. Like a mouse running the squeaky wheel. You are NEVER going to find serenity in this environment. It's like looking for a needle in a haystack.

What is serenity or calmness worth to you? Does it have any value? Yes. It is, in fact, priceless.

Guess what? In our society we have lost respect for serenity and calmness of mind. Why? Because it means moving more slowly and more reflectively. Because it doesn't fit in with the thoughtless values that currently pervade our minds and it doesn't follow the paradigm our parents and others passed on to us: get ahead, beat the other person, the early bird gets the worm, it's a jungle out there, etc. We leave our homes each morning headed for that frantic urban, even global environment and we are ALREADY wired before the day starts!

But let's continue to think for a moment about what this truly means for us in our lives. Let's go back to the streets. Look at the person who is on drugs or the person who has mental health issues. Can they have serenity and calmness in their lives? No--NEVER. Why not? Because their minds are always racing in overdrive. They are bombarded with frantic thoughts: "Where do I get my next hit? Why did she say that to me? Why didn't I do it this way? I don't like feeling like this--I'd rather feel numb. I am so confused!"

You cannot get inside of minds like these but you can see that they have NO serenity and no calmness available to them even when they find a quiet moment on their own; their minds remain hyperactive and disturbed. Their minds are ever racing in an out-of-control fast forward. And they are addicted to this feeling. They believe that this is the only way they can live. Drugged up, mindless, confused and afraid - they know no other way.

Do you believe that the only way you can live with your mind is the way that you are thinking right now, at this moment? That the way your mind functions now is so much better than the minds that I have just described to you? So, basically, you are ok because you do not live at THAT level of frenzied activity.

Well, I would say that you need to think about that and reflect on these words by one of my favorite authors, James Allen:

> *Calmness of mind is one of the beautiful jewels of wisdom.*
> *It is a result of long and patient effort in self-control.*
> *Its presence is an indication of ripened experience, and of a more than ordinary knowledge of the law and operations of thought.*
>
> James Allen

This takes practice. It is not a snap decision. You cannot snap your fingers and be there. Discovering calmness of mind is a skill. You must work for it. You must continually practice to achieve it.

There is NO reason why, when you have truly reflected and thought about your own practice, you cannot decide to speed up what you are doing in a *healthy* way and yet calm down inside. That is, to seek serenity in your life.

When you begin the practice of a serene and calm life, amazing things will begin to happen for you. Suddenly, "all the pieces" will fall into place. Your life will begin to flow in a way that creates a positive momentum for you and each and every day. Others will begin to notice the change in you, too.

Your initial reaction may be negative: that it's not possible! You can't live *without* fighting! You *have to* scratch and claw for every advantage. I must *absolutely* get ahead of everyone else! These comments, in truth, are your ego at its worst. Are you listening? *ALL of these excuses are your ego at its worst!*

How do you get past this negative attitude?

Think of the ocean. When you are on the surface, riding the waves, you are subject to the conditions of the weather. The sky is blue or overcast or dark. The winds are slight or up to gale force. As you live your life in this ocean, you are forever adrift. You are tossed about depending upon the sea conditions guaranteed! You have no control.

But there is a deeper part of the ocean where the waves and the gale force winds have NO impact whatsoever. The water remains calm and serene despite the horrible and unsettling conditions that exist above the surface, in the air. If you have always lived your life on the surface of, say, the North Atlantic Ocean, a storm-tossed sea, it may not seem possible that there is a much calmer place beneath the waves in which you can live your life. But there is.

Deep inside, our higher Self knows that this is true, though. What your mind sometimes does not know is how to get there, to these calm seas. This is where your inner GPS comes into play and guides you to that place deeper in the ocean where calmness of mind and serenity wash over you each and every day. Not only have you then a terrific feeling of peace inside, but also you allow your fears to subside and wash away so that you can live every day expecting the best, intending the best, manifesting the best.

Let's take a look at the greatest hurdle to success: FEAR.

What is fear anyway? I like this acronym for fear: False Expectations Appearing Real.

If you consider what you were afraid of one year ago, what do you discover? Probably that none of those fears came true. Most fear is irrational to begin with and only serves to stop you in your tracks from making progress. That little voice in your head that suddenly appears and shouts at you, "Who do you think you are? You're crazy. You can't do that! Your world will fall apart if you do that. You'll be a failure!" and other such nonsense. And it is nonsense. You MUST learn right now to shut that voice up and tell it to get the hell out of your life.

Fear causes more issues than you realize. You have to face those fears and move through them. I like what Brian Tracy says: "If you face your fear, the death of fear is certain." I really like that.

How about you? What do you do when fear rears its ugly head? Do you take action and move through it or do you retreat back into safety to avoid facing it? It is a place of false security. It is good for the moment only. It is avoidance behavior and does not help you break through.

It's a fascinating question and one that makes you think. You MUST bother to think about it. You definitely need to reflect on this in order to consider more healthy ways to deal with your fear and anxiety and, thus, achieve a calmer, more serene life.

> *How many people we know who sour their lives,*
> *who ruin all that is sweet and beautiful by explosive tempers,*
> *who destroy their poise of character, and make bad blood!*
> *It is a question whether the great majority of people do not*
> *ruin their lives and mar their happiness by lack of self-control.*
> *How few people we meet in life who are well-balanced,*
> *who have that exquisite poise which is characteristic*
> *of the finished character!*
>
> James Allen

It is not how hard you try or how long you work. It is how effortlessly you get more of the right things done that makes all the difference. You cannot do things in an easy and effortless manner without calmness of mind. All of that conflict we've been talking about--competition, plotting, gossiping, and disease takes up a tremendous amount of useless mind energy. It gets you nowhere and goes nowhere good.

If you look at this in terms of ALL the potential mind energy available to one person being devoted to crap and disturbance, you will begin to understand precisely what you are wasting. You are wasting your precious mind and your precious life on thoughts that debilitate you and prevent you from EVER achieving the success you dream of.

Why are you doing this? It makes no sense at all and deep inside you know it.

A large part of the path to changing this woeful condition involves having a healthy respect and belief in gratitude. Gratitude for what you have. Gratitude for where you are. Gratitude for how life is going right now for you – the good and the bad. Gratitude is SO IMPORTANT. This does not mean you want to continue to live in the way you are living now, or that you are satisfied with where you are in your career or your relationships – possibly you are unhappy with certain things in your life. In order to move forward in your life in a positive manner, you MUST be grateful for everything you currently have in your life in order to begin to clear you mind and position yourself to have more GPS, MORE Growth, Prosperity and Success.

By making room in your thoughts, by letting go of your fears and by being grateful, you free up so much more mind space to help you get a step-up to your next level. It is waiting for you now with your new-found awareness and growth. Interestingly enough, this will help you to calm down inside, and speed up in your effectiveness every day. Embrace your Growth Principle: Serenity!

Think of this power as something that you can connect with at any time. It has the answer to all your problems. It offers you freedom from fear, from worry, from sickness, from accident. No man and no thing can interfere with your use of this power or diminish your share of it. No one, that is, but yourself.
Robert Collier

Chapter Seven

Growth Principle – Success

The difference between the successful man and the unsuccessful one is not so much a matter of training or equipment. It is not a question of opportunity or luck. It is just in the way they, each of them, look at things. The successful man sees an opportunity, seizes upon it, and moves upward another rung on the ladder of success. It never occurs to him that he may fail. He sees only the opportunity, he visions what he can do with it, and all the forces within and without him combine to help him win.

Robert Collier

If you take a moment and look about you in nature you see tremendous, ongoing, awesome success everywhere you look – if you look for it. You cannot glance or say, "Oh, yeah, I know." You have to take the time to look and see. It's more than just humanity. We are not the only life on the Earth. It is NOT an accident – profusion and abundance exist all around us in nature and continue to renew and advance right in front of us. How does this happen? Well, without getting technical about it, obviously there is a plan that works and it works every time.

The profusion of nature claims its space in the world and does so in an ongoing, continuous manner whether we choose to notice it or not! It is what nature does. It, life and success, has been doing this for millions of years. As you are part of nature, part of this earth, you have the same capacity within you! You can claim your space but only by looking for and projecting the positive regenerative, timeless qualities within yourself. You must learn to continue to claim your space in the world in an ongoing and continuous manner – quietly, easily, efficiently and effectively. This takes energy and focus.

If it appears to you that no one is noticing you – that does not matter. Your perception is probably wrong. Then, having determined to go ahead, thinking that you can move forward when people notice what you are doing, you put yourself in a negative space. For you find you *need* others to notice you and, so, you only work when you're being watched or think others are watching. That is your ego interfering with your own growth process. The lazy person's ego is a highway to a low quality destination. Turn your ego down – preferably *off*. Keep working on your own success at all times. Every day, every way, it gets a little better when you choose to head in the direction of your GPS Millionaire.

Many people like to think, for whatever reason, that they 'can't' do something. They claim a negative position for themselves before the race has even started. *Can't* is one of the worst four-letter words in the English language! As an educator, I have seen many former students over the years that had incredible challenges in front of them, compared to everyone else. People with physical disabilities, mental challenges, and health issues face challenges that affect their performance. As the able-bodied see it, these people have limitations that are seen as daunting and insurmountable. They would make most people feel like they just wanted to quit. The physically and mentally challenged don't quit. They overcome enormous difficulties that would stop most of us dead in our tracks. They simply do things differently. They adjust their attitude in a BIG way – and continue on – blind teachers, disabled athletes, and hearing-impaired workers. All sorts of people never stopped – they rose to the challenge, created changes and moved on in the world. Here lies the truth to success: you must never quit! It's ok to think about it, it's fine to talk about it – just don't do it!

I have worked with thousands of young people, teenagers who often felt the weight of failure or a lack of self-confidence, and sometimes they said to me, "Sir, I can't do that!" In those instances, I connected them with an individual who had far more serious physical or health issues and afterwards asked them: "Now, who do you think the teacher is more inclined to believe when they say, 'I can't' – you or the person you just met?" I'd be more inclined to believe the latter. Why? Because when you listen to them you realize that they are achieving success in their lives because of their willingness not to quit against all odds. They did NOT quit! They put everything they've got into making a better life for themselves and for those around them! So why do you think it's ok for you to feel that you *can't* put your mind behind doing the work of living up your potential? Why do you feel that you have permission to just let things go and easily quit when the going seems to get tough for you? Why do you feel that the solution for you when you run up against an apparent barrier is to quit? Guess what? This is a copout!!

I'd like you to meet a friend of mine right now – he is an amazing man who had been through challenges that would make most people wilt under that pressure. His name is Rodney Flowers and he is from Maryland. I am grateful to be able to call him my friend. After a devastating injury on a tackle playing football in high school, he found himself unable to move his legs – he was paralyzed. He was told many times by doctors that he would never be able to walk again and that his life was to be forever changed. He faced innumerable challenges, both physical and emotional, along the way in seeking to regain his health. His life *was* changed forever. But did he quit? I am sure he thought about it, and probably talked about it. I am also sure that it was NOT easy for him. But did he DO it? NO – most certainly not!! You can visit his website to learn more about his journey and his inspiring devotion to sharing his "Get Up!" message with thousands and thousands around the world. Rodney Flowers is an amazing man and a great friend of mine. A true success in life, Rodney Flowers has what it takes. Visit www.rodneyflowers.com for more information.

But the *can'ts* to success come from everywhere – inside you and outside you. For instance, the boy who was told he was too stupid to get a four-year college degree. He not only didn't listen to those negative voices by achieving that goal, he now has a PhD. because he chose to set his sights even higher. How many people do you know who were told "You can't do that!" then went out and did that and even achieved something better? They beat the odds, too. They made a success of their lives. They didn't give up in the face of negativity and neither should you!

Take a moment now and consider those times in your life when you felt most successful. What happened? How did you feel? What were the results? Results are the key to success. Unless you can measure the difference your success has made, you are only dreaming or wishing. Nothing wrong with dreaming or wishing – but to turn those dreams and wishes into great success you have to take action and apply yourself and the only proof of your efforts is in your results. You have to put down the remote, get up off the couch and take action on something you are passionate about so you can move your idea of success forward. To test your dream, your passionate desire fully in the world, to see whether it will bring you the results you are looking forward to.

Don't be discouraged if this process doesn't work on the first try. This is an issue for people who are thinking about quitting from the get-go. They have decided, in advance, that their attempt at success is not going to work anyway. So, in order to be right, they use the effort and work put into attempting to make their idea a success, as a REASON for claiming afterward, "You see? I knew it wouldn't work!"

What a horrible thing to do with the glorious original idea that you came up with. Why would you ever want to come up with another idea, when "I know it's not going to work" is the silent, underlying attitude you have to begin with and your resulting thought is, "You see? I knew it wouldn't work anyway!" This is a plan going nowhere, a recipe for disaster. You are actually going in circles in your thinking and will NEVER produce a successful outcome. You must take 100% responsibility and make a 100% commitment to making your idea a reality--and DO NOT STOP until that is the result you achieve NO MATTER WHAT!!

When you fully achieved the great moments of success in your life what happened? I am sure that you felt wonderful, fully alive and excited that the things you were planning were manifesting for you in exciting and bountiful ways. You felt passionate about your purpose! In some ways, you "knew" what you were doing was going to produce great success, even though it had not yet appeared in physical form. And when it did, you felt great! You felt powerful!

This is the way you want to live every day of your life!!

We have an innate desire to endlessly learn, grow, and develop. We want to become more than what we already are. Once we yield to this inclination for continuous and never-ending improvement, we lead a life of endless accomplishments and satisfaction.
                                        Jack Canfield, *The Success Principles*

You must understand that success is a CHOICE. You must make the decision that you are going to be successful and then stick with it until you are. See yourself with easy, massive success. Visualize your success. Create pictures in your mind that help you to see it more clearly, just as athletes do before competition. The more clearly you see your success and what that looks like, the more quickly you will be able to manifest it through applying yourself. When you do so, you will be amazed at how your success takes form for you. It may not even be

EXACTLY the way you envisioned it. It will be BETTER in ways that you hadn't even thought of.

That is the power of the Growth Principle – Success. It engages your inner GPS – your inner Global Positioning System – and sets it towards Growth, Prosperity and Success! Can you see the power of my GPS brand and the metaphor behind it? Metaphors have GREAT power and can help you to understand what YOU have to do to achieve massive success. They can unleash the power of your subconscious mind working for you, helping you to unlock the Secret of the Ages for the 21st Century!

Study it. Work with it. Develop your own success principles and goals that take you on your journey to the stars. Maybe you have already started. Perhaps you are already achieving a higher degree of success than your peers. It really does not matter where you are on the ladder of success that Robert Collier described above – you must remind yourself continuously about these ideas. You must study them every day and be grateful for what you already have in your life. You must GET UP and GET MOVING toward your goals. If you do that every day, my GPS tells me that you will eventually arrive at your destination.

The speed of your journey is one thing, but it is setting off in the right DIRECTION that makes ALL the difference. Make a commitment to set your direction right now – because when you are heading in a SUCCESS direction life will seem to flow naturally and easily to you. You will KNOW that you are heading in the right direction – your health will improve, your relationships will be great, your finances will improve and your LIFE will become clearer.

This is the power of using your inner GPS – it propels you forward in the most exciting and natural way. It supports you fully in achieving your goal of becoming a GPS Millionaire. Go for it. You will Love it!!

The first principle of success is desire – knowing what you want. Desire is the planting of the seed.
Robert Collier

Chapter Eight

Grander Personal Surprises

There is no philosophy by which a person can do a thing when he thinks he can't. The reasons why millions of people are plodding along in mediocrity today, many of them barely making a living, when they have the ability to do something infinitely bigger, is because they lack confidence in themselves. They don't believe they can do the bigger thing that would lift them out of their rut of mediocrity and poverty, they are not winners mentally. ...It is the victorious mental attitude, the consciousness of power, the sense of mastership, that does the big things in this world. If you haven't this attitude, if you lack self-confidence, begin now to cultivate it.

Robert Collier

No one knows everything – it just isn't possible. In today's data-rich world of the 21st Century, we are swimming in a sea of information. Much of the information we have in front of us has no value at all, or it is wrong. So, we spend considerable time searching the internet; and, also, hanging out on Facebook and social media; watching TV and movies; reading news articles and magazines – busy, busy, busy – searching for relevant and useful information. This is a TOTAL waste of time and energy.

Henry Ford was sued, at one time, for not being smart enough! Wow! Can you imagine? The lawyer examining Henry Ford was asking him a whole series of silly questions designed to test his knowledge and demonstrate his lack of it. When Mr. Ford replied by saying, "I may not know the answer to this question or all of the other silly questions you have been asking me, however, I have buttons on my desk at my disposal that I can press at any time to connect me with people that can give me the answers to these silly questions and to many, many more that you haven't even thought of." The court spectators erupted in laughter at the questioning lawyer.

Mr. Ford had shown with his answer not only an intelligence beyond the scope of that lawyer and his silly questions, he clearly demonstrated that he was, in fact, a highly intelligent individual who knew how to select and focus on the information that was critical to achieving his goals.

Today, almost a hundred years later, life is no different. Even though we are awash in information everywhere we turn, it is still up to us to select what we focus on, and what we give our attention to. Why is that? Well, if you think for a moment you will realize that whatever you focus on, whatever you give your attention to GROWS! It expands and gets bigger. You come out with more specific information than you went looking for.

That is WHY it is SO important for you to choose wisely what you focus on and what you give your attention to. You already know that when you do so, it will expand and grow. So it is MOST important that you select positive, inspiring and outstanding information, since that will expand and grow the positive, the inspiring and the outstanding in your life! It is really that simple.

When you choose to become involved in negative, energy-draining situations that pull you down and destroy your self-confidence, you are actually attracting and growing MORE of those situations to yourself. You're growing weeds, not flowers. This is NOT a good thing. It is NOT the way to connect and grow your inner GPS Millionaire!

Plus, while you are being thrown off track and your thinking becomes scattered and downgraded, you are actually missing the positive and uplifting opportunities that are right in front of you. You cannot see them because your energy is being pulled into the negative, energy-draining situation, which then grows larger.

It can even cause you to become attracted to more energy-draining situations until you are drowning. This means, logically, that while you are focusing on the negative – you cannot see the opportunities that may even be right in front of you.

Shocking, isn't it? Can you think of one or two examples in your life where that has happened to you? This is when you know for sure that you are on the wrong path. You have closed the door on opportunity, because your mind energy is occupied with thoughtless, mindless negativity, and you are not in a position to focus on Grander Personal Surprises.

That is what makes life interesting and worthwhile – having opportunities that present themselves to you so that you can take advantage of them. When you live your life as a GPS Millionaire, you search out Grander Personal Surprises, and when they come, you grab them and take advantage of them. They are yours to enjoy and grow with on your road to success!

It is through taking action that you manifest more capacity in yourself; without action all the capacity you may possess is useless. Once you begin to act on the things that matter to you, even by making the smallest change in your viewpoint or behavior, space in your mind or psychological daylight magically opens up for you.

Your mind has the capacity to sense, reflect, and create ideas continually; but there's a huge difference between imagining a fulfilling life and actually living it. Every aspect of the brightest future you envision, the best relationships you desire, and the most energy you deserve for life depends on your taking action along the road leading toward the end you have in mind – becoming a GPS Millionaire.

When you are on this road to your inner GPS, it changes your mind, causing it to pause along the way to reflect and wonder about what you actually care about, not merely what the world tells you to care about, but what you care about.

In time of change, the learners will inherit the Earth, while the learned find themselves beautifully equipped to live in a world that no longer exists.

Eric Hoffer

To find the Grander Personal Surprises ahead for you, make your best effort to seek more clarity by doing some or all of the following:

1. Follow your own dreams, not someone else's. Yes, you will encounter disappointments along the way; life will NOT follow your script most of the time. The truth is that a mind that has not faced and taken 100% responsibility for

disappointment and found unique and novel ways to deal with it is not nearly as resourceful as one that has. Imitation is not knowledge. So, go for YOUR dreams. Make them happen!

2. Avoid impulsive behavior, overriding it with character. Research has shown that when we have to consider long-range goals and plans, our thinking is basically rational because our logical reasoning can win the day over our emotions. We can calmly face important decisions in our lives that seem far off in the distance. But, when we are faced with a choice right now to devour something appealing to us right away or to delay gratification by not doing so, we are often more higgledy-piggledy than our family pets. Research has shown that holding off on impulsive behavior like this is absolutely vital to sustained success in life and work.

3. Yet you cannot forget that your heart is in all of this. Check to see that your heart is with you – that your heart is invested in what you are doing. Often we close down our other ways of knowing and rely totally on our logical reasoning to make our business and personal decisions because we often want to rely on what is rationally knowable. This would be a HUGE mistake! You have to learn to include your widest range of intuition and instincts – your intellectual factors –

to help you understand your world to make your best decisions in any situation. When your heart is touched by a situation, it changes how you look on it. We know that this is true and when it happens, it defies what is rationally knowable. Imagine how successful you could become if your heart was involved in absolutely every choice and decision you had to make in life – you probably would NEVER go wrong.

4. Select something that 'can't be done' and go and do it. Change the 'can't' to 'can!'

Remember, I told you one of the worst four-letter words in the English language is the word 'can't.' How many times as young person you told were, "You can't do that!" Think about it for a moment. You want to revisit some of those ideas that are still in your mind. Maybe you were told 'no' about things that are very near and dear to your heart. Is it time to change a can't to a can? You bet! Go for it!

5. Don't look for the accolades! Sometimes we spend too much time in our lives seeking credit. Ignoring the team and those who put us in a position to succeed, we blow it by letting our ego rule the day in our life. Again, another big mistake! Don't do it for the trophy! Do it because it is the right thing to do and you are passionate about doing your best and

always doing the right thing. You will see your life shift in a big way if you follow this advice.

Minimizing your ego is the BEST solution in almost every situation. Why? Because our ego makes bad choices for us. It leads us down the path of unhealthy competition and exclusion, through creating harmful feelings of superiority over others. You are no better and no worse than anyone else. The more you can do to sing the praises of the people, the team members and the leaders who supported your success, the more success you will have! You will have opened yourself up for more and more Grander Personal Surprises of the BEST kind!!!

6. Live what you believe and make your obstacles into stepping stones!

Stay calm! Don't let your obstacles grow into massive, immovable objects that exist only in your mind. Don't take things personally or create conflict at any time. Be your best Self! Focus forward and work to tone down the very reactive components of your mind and free yourself up to those areas in your life that are seeking GPS (Growth, Prosperity and Success!).

7. Always seek clarity. When assessing the obstacles you perceive inside, and your reactions to those perceived obstacles, understand that you are seeing them from a very narrow perspective. Your mind has a strong desire to see what you are looking for. The more you know or think you know about a situation, the more blinded you can become to what is actually happening. By narrowing your perspective, you diminish ALL the good that you are capable of doing. Remember, you should always be seeking MORE capacity, not less. Do not fall into this trap! Seek clarity – the truth will set you free! Remember the words of Pulitzer Prize-winning author, Daniel Boorstin, who wrote, "The greatest obstacle to progress is not ignorance, but the illusion of knowledge."

8. Know that you can do it! The key difference between lucky and unlucky people is that lucky people embrace changes in habits and new experiences. In fact, they don't just embrace it, they actively seek it out. They do this in several ways – by embracing the new and changing at least one routine every day. They trust their heart and stomach more and listen to their intuition about things. They build trust relationships that are deep and meaningful and they use their imagination and creativity to build an idea in their mind to follow their dreams to become a GPS Millionaire!

Following the principles outlined in this chapter will cause you to experience Grander Personal Surprises in your life. Your inner GPS will guide you on the right path to a life of excitement and change that will energize and empower you to move forward on your journey. Making these commitments to receiving Grander Personal Surprises will enervate your spirit and cause you to look out on the world with a new found respect and joy for everything that the universe has brought and is bringing your way. Life will get better and better for you if you study and apply these GPS Millionaire principles.

Cultivate confidence in yourself. Cultivate the feeling that you ARE succeeding. Know that you have unlimited power to do every right thing. Know that with Universal Mind to draw upon, no position is too difficult, and no problem too hard.

Robert Collier

Chapter Nine

Goals Predict Success

Remember this: The Universal Mind is omnipotent. And when the subconscious mind is in tune with the Higher Self, there is no limit to the things that it can do. Given any desire that is in harmony with the Universal Mind, and you have but to hold that desire in your thought with confident and serene faith to attract from the invisible domain the things you need to satisfy it. You see, there is just as much of the Creative Force around you today as there was when the world was made.

Robert Collier

Your inner GPS is your Higher Self – reaching and striving for growth, prosperity and success is what it does because what you nurture and believe grows. It expands both in you and in your world. If you look around you in nature for a moment, you cannot help but see growth, prosperity and success everywhere you look. Nature creates no failures – it creates things that grow and grow in abundance everywhere. Abundance is our natural state on earth. Embrace it and share it.

One of the most famous documents in the history of mankind, *The Upanishads*, states "From abundance, he took abundance, and still abundance remained." You are here on this earth to grow, and you can never take more than your share. You must set goals to live in the reality of your abundance. Most people approach the ocean of success timidly with a teaspoon, or a thimble, hoping to get a little bit for themselves, maybe. This is wrong thinking that actually causes your mind to atrophy and become more rigid in its functioning. You must think Growth, Prosperity and Success !

Just a few of the right minutes applied in the right way every day to creating the future will allow you to capture more and more of the opportunities that otherwise you would have missed. Let areas of the forebrain atrophy because you fail to stimulate them to envision the future, and you automatically invisibly, deep in your brain's structure, become more rigid and rule-anchored, unable to change. You get mired in old habits and limitations, less able to survive change, let alone dream big and make those dreams into realities. You know people like this, and now you know why, no matter what you do, you can't get them genuinely excited about a better, different future, or truly engaged in building such a future.

Robert K. Cooper, PhD.

Goals, BIG Goals, not only stimulate and expand and grow your thinking; they create a better life for you and your friends and family. You must set goals that excite, challenge and scare you all at the same time. This is why the question of what you want is so vitally important. You will never pursue big goals unless you can articulate why you want them in your life. You must want what you want passionately, believing in your ability and talent to achieve it, declaring your desire fully. You must be ALL IN! It is NOT a goal if you think you *might* like to *maybe* have something, if that is ok with someone else. Sound the buzzer – HONK!!! No goal!! You Lose!!

Setting goals is strictly a process between you and yourself – no one else is involved in this process. You must set your goals on your own. Yes, other people come into play as you pursue your goals – but their OPINION of what your goals should be are just that – their Opinion! Most people spend way too much time thinking about the opinions of others and they are often devastated when someone they care about or respect makes a negative remark, or a 'put-down' about what they want to do with their life.

Here's the truth: it is no one else's business what you want to do with your life! It's your business! What other people 'think' of you and your ideas is NOT your business. Forget it! Let it go! Keeping reaching and striving for goals that you are 100% passionate about and do not concern yourself with what other people think.

Just continue to do what you believe in and what you are committed to achieving in your own life. Do you know what those people will say when you have achieved your goal and are demonstrating huge success in the world? They will say things like, "I always knew he would be a success at that!" "She always was dedicated to doing that amazing work. Isn't she great?" Believe it or not, what they will say when you are a success will be different from what you are hearing from them now. So...guess what? What they say now about your goals and your life DOES NOT MATTER!! Don't waste any more time thinking about it.

No matter how carefully you plan your goals they will never be more than pipe dreams unless you pursue them with gusto.
W. Clement Stone

Passion, commitment, persistence, faith and belief are what count most in bringing your goals into reality. When you make a 100% commitment to a goal, you are all in. You bring your passion for what you are seeking into play. You are willing to do whatever it takes to make it happen. This is the exact opposite of those who try to achieve what they want by saying what they don't want. You know these folks – "I want this, but I don't want this or that or this and that, etc." They never achieve their goals!!

You have to be passionate and committed to what you want! Then, to that, you add your faith in your unique abilities and talents to produce the result that you are seeking, that you dreamed about. You mix it in with the belief that you have the mindset and the confidence to earn and deserve the success you are seeking. You keep persisting every day in moving closer to your goals. What can you do each day that moves you closer to your goals? You know that you care, you know that you are willing to serve and you know that your goal is about helping others to be successful in their lives – because your success is dependent on those qualities inside you: your inner GPS. It is NOT about competing, beating, or harming other people in any way. You always strive to work cooperatively, harmoniously, productively with others in a way that is dedicated to your passion, commitment, persistence, faith and belief. You are then on target to your goal of becoming a GPS Millionaire!

Your chances of success in any undertaking can always be measured by your belief in yourself.
Robert Collier

Let me ask you a question that can truly change the way you think about goals. Do you have 100 Goals that can change your life?

I do. I can proudly say that "My 100 Goals can Change My Life!"

You might answer, "Really? Why should I care about having 100 Goals?"

Good question. Let me tell you why –

On January 30, 2005 I wrote out 100 Goals for my life on a sheet of paper. I probably reviewed them for a month or so after that, I really don't recall exactly. But I do know that I put that sheet away in a binder in my files later in the spring of 2005.

"So what?" you might say, "I'm looking to get some help in my life right now – not from a long time ago!"

Give me a chance to explain.

Fast forward with me now to mid-December in 2015 – just a short while ago. I'm going through my old files and I come across my List of 100 Goals from January 30, 2005. At that point, almost 11 years ago!

I decided to spend some time reviewing what I had put down on the list to see whether I had accomplished any of the 100 Goals I had listed way back when. There were travel goals, wealth goals, family goals, career goals, health and relationship goals, and more. My Life Goals from that time in 2005!

Are you with me on this? This can really help you, if you are paying close attention.

I reviewed my results, as of December 2015, from my list from January 30, 2005. What did I discover? I learned that I had achieved close to 90% of my goals on that 2005 List!! 90% - Isn't that AMAZING? I was stunned. There in my hands, right in front of me, was PROOF that I had the ability to set goals and achieve them in a BIG way in my life.

What did I do with this information after the amazement I felt had diminished? I sat right down in early January 2016 and wrote out a NEW list of 100 Goals that I was seeking to achieve in my life.

Here is what I would recommend MOST STRONGLY to you! – Get a sheet of paper and a pen. Sit down with a cup of tea or coffee (your favorite calming beverage!) on your own in a quiet space. Write out your own 100 Goals! Go nuts – put down anything and everything you would LOVE to do, be, or have in your life right now and you will be AMAZED at the results you achieve later on down the road, as I was.

Now – I am NOT suggesting that you wait 10-11 years to check in and see how you are doing. I think it would be important to check in more frequently than I did. Perhaps do a yearly review of your list, or review it every 2-3 years to update and change it going forward. This will bring massive GPS Millionaire success into your life – so get on it RIGHT NOW!!! It is the most productive thing that you can do to change your life in a BIG way.

Once the list is done – put it away in a safe place where you can return at any time to review it. Do not share it with anyone – it is strictly between you and yourself. Of course, you may want to share some of it with your spouse or partner – but make sure before you share it, that anyone you share it with is supportive and enthused to see you achieving the success you desire!

Now you can see, from the experience I shared with you, why Goals Predict Success! It happens every time, for every person that follows these principles. You can do it! Go for it and make it happen!

If you don't make things happen then things will happen to you. Take the first step, and your mind will mobilize all its forces to your aid. But the first essential is that you begin. Once the battle is started, all that is within and without you will come to your assistance. Visualize this thing that you want, see it, feel it, believe in it. Make your mental blue print and begin to build.

Robert Collier

Chapter Ten

Great People Surround

Initiative, plus imagination, will take you anywhere. Imagination opens the eye of the mind, and there is nothing good you can image there that is not possible of fulfillment in your daily life.

The connecting link between the human and the Divine, between the formed universe and the formless energy, lies in your imaging faculty. ...Through it we share in the creative power of Universal Mind.

It is the means by which we avail ourselves of all the good which Universal Mind is constantly offering to us in such profusion. It is the means by which we can reach any goal, win any prize.

Robert Collier

The Great People that Surround us and have come here before us have provided a rich legacy of learning and information that we are blessed to be able to benefit from and use in our lives right now! This is a BIG idea that was referenced by a giant of his time in the world – Sir Isaac Newton. He said, in a letter he wrote in 1676 speaking of his outstanding achievements, "If I have seen further it is by standing on the shoulders of the Giants that have gone before me."

We should always remember that we don't have to re-invent the wheel, as we may sometimes believe. We can learn and then stand on the shoulders of the giants who have gone before us. By doing so, not only will we learn the timeless truths of the ages, we will also be able to see further into the future to build and expand on the ideas and knowledge that we have been given by those giants.

This is the Secret of the Ages for the 21st Century! Here are eight of my personal giants – I have learned SO MUCH from them and love standing on their shoulders to have a clearer view of the GPS Millionaire road in front of me. I am truly GRATEFUL and appreciate so much that Great People Surround Us! You can join us: study their lives and their work and you, too, will be able to Surround yourself with Great People and improve your own life starting from today!!

1. **James Allen (1864-1912)**
   James Allen was an English Author born of poor circumstances whose mother could neither read nor write. His father, unfortunately, was believed to have been murdered when he died tragically only one day after

arriving in New York City, travelling ahead on his own of his family to seek a better life for them. James Allen's second book, *As A Man Thinketh*, was his most influential. *As A Man Thinketh* was written over 100 years ago but still continues to deliver a timeless wisdom to those who study and apply the principles of life it teaches. Here are some quotes:

"Circumstances do not make the man, they reveal him."

"The more tranquil a man becomes, the greater is his success, his influence, his power for good. Calmness of mind is one of the beautiful jewels of wisdom."

"For true success ask yourself these four questions: Why? Why not? Why not me? Why not now?"

"You are today where your thoughts have brought you; you will be tomorrow where your thoughts take you."

2. **Andrew Carnegie (1835-1919)**

Andrew Carnegie was the richest man in the world at the end of the 19th century. In addition to being a self-made GPS multimillionaire who was born of poor circumstances in Scotland, Andrew Carnegie had a deep desire to share the principles of success that he learned and used to achieve great heights in order to teach others the science of

successful living – a new idea at that time. His goal in life was to earn as much as possible until the age of 50, then to use the remainder of his life to give it all away. Andrew Carnegie introduced Napoleon Hill to his concept of success and inspired him to dedicate his life to researching and promoting that information to the world. There are still innumerable examples of the generosity of Andrew Carnegie. You need look no further than the public library for his influence on the thinking of our world (the public library is only one idea that he gave to the masses in North America). Not many people realize that not only did Carnegie fund the building of libraries in the United States, he did so all over the world, including in Canada. Here is a website link to a listing of ALL of the libraries funded by Andrew Carnegie in Canada:
http://www.mtc.gov.on.ca/en/libraries/carnegie.shtml

Here are some quotes from Andrew Carnegie:

"A person wanting to advance must do something exceptional. They must attract attention."

"Do not look for approval except for the consciousness of doing your best."

"The person who acquires the ability to take full possession of his own mind may take possession of anything else to which they are justly entitled."

"Think of yourself as on the threshold of unparalleled success. A whole, clear, glorious life lies before you. Achieve! Achieve!"

3. **Robert Collier (1885-1950)**

    A personal favorite of ours, Robert Collier was an American author of metaphysical books in the 20th century. His quotes and thoughts are highlighted throughout GPS Millionaire in EVERY chapter permeating every page with his classic GPS wisdom! He was the nephew of the founder of the publication – *Collier's Weekly*. He was involved in writing, editing, and research for most of his life. His book *The Secret of the Ages* (1925) sold over 300,000 copies during his life and is considered a classic by many. Collier wrote about the practical psychology of abundance, desire, faith, visualization, confident action, and becoming your best.

    Here are some additional Robert Collier quotes:

    "There is little difference in people, but that little difference makes a big difference. That little difference is attitude. The big difference is whether it is positive or negative."

"All riches have their origin in mind. Wealth is in ideas - not money."

"Playing safe is probably the most unsafe thing in the world. You cannot stand still. You must go forward."

"See the things you want as already yours. Think of them as yours, as belonging to you, as already in your possession."

4. **Napoleon Hill (1883-1970)**

He is widely considered to be one of the great writers on success in life. His most famous work, *Think & Grow Rich* (1937), is one of the best-selling books of all time (at the time of Hill's death in 1970, *Think and Grow Rich* had sold 20 million copies). Hill's works examined the power of personal beliefs, and the role they play in personal success. He became an advisor to President Franklin D. Roosevelt from 1933 to 1936. Hill's views on the philosophy of success are widely held and still used today to influence and inspire people to think about their own personal success journey.

Here are some Napoleon Hill quotes:

"Every adversity, every failure, every heartache carries with it the seed on an equal or greater benefit."

"All the breaks you need in life wait within your imagination; Imagination is the workshop of your mind, capable of turning mind energy into accomplishment and wealth."

"Most great people have attained their greatest success just one step beyond their greatest failure."

"Great achievement is usually born of great sacrifice, and is never the result of selfishness."

5. **Earl Nightingale (1921-1989)**
Earl Nightingale was an American motivational speaker and author, known as the "Dean of Personal Development." When Nightingale was seventeen he joined the Marine Corps. He was on the USS Arizona during the Japanese attack on Pearl Harbour on December 7, 1941 and was one of twelve surviving Marines on board that day. After the war, Nightingale began to work in the radio industry, which eventually led to work as a motivational speaker. In 1956 he produced a spoken word record, *The Strangest Secret,* which sold over a million copies, making it the first spoken-word recording to achieve Gold Record status. Earl was also one of the founding partners, along with Lloyd Conant, of the largest personal development corporation in the world –

Nightingale-Conant Corp. Earl Nightingale mentored MANY successful people, most notably Bob Proctor.

"Learn to enjoy every minute of your life. Be happy now. Don't wait for something outside of yourself to make you happy in the future. Think how really precious is the time you have to spend, whether it's at work or with your family. Every minute should be enjoyed and savored."

"The biggest mistake that you can make is to believe that you are working for somebody else. Job security is gone. The driving force of a career must come from the individual. Remember: Jobs are owned by the company; you own your career!"

"Success is the progressive realization of a worthy goal or ideal."

6. **Bob Proctor (1934 -   )**

Bob Proctor was born in Owen Sound, Ontario, Canada. He is a master motivator, inspirational speaker and author of several books including the best seller *You Were Born Rich*. His main inspiration comes from Napoleon Hill's *Think and Grow Rich*. Proctor is a high school dropout who worked a series of part time and low paying jobs early in his life and owed more than he earned until age 26. Proctor notes that within a year of reading Hill's book, he was earning over $100,000 per year. Bob then moved to Chicago to work with his real-life mentor, Earl Nightingale. After rising to the position of Vice President of Sales at Nightingale-Conant Corporation, he established his own seminar company. Proctor now travels the world giving his seminars and selling his books and programs helping others. Bob Proctor gained worldwide exposure for his appearance in the hit film the 'The Secret' which revealed how to apply the law of attraction to gain success in all areas of a person's life. After becoming Vice President of Sales at Nightingale-Conant, Bob Proctor founded Life Success Productions. Proctor became partners with Sandra Gallagher in 2009 when they co-developed the *Thinking Into Results* Program. He is now Chairman and Co-Founder of the Proctor Gallagher Institute, a company offering personal growth seminars, selling programs that include learning opportunities for coaching, masterminding and consulting to people around the world.

You can learn more about Bob Proctor at: www.proctorgallagherinstitute.com

Here are some quotes from Bob Proctor:

"No amount of reading or memorizing will make you successful in life. It is the understanding and application of wise thought that counts."

"See yourself living in abundance and you will attract it. It always works; it works every time with every person."

"Everything you are seeking is seeking you. Therefore, everything you want is already yours. So, you don't have to get anything. It is simply a matter of becoming more aware of what you already possess."

"Thoughts become things. If you can see it in your mind, you will hold it in your hand."

7. **Jim Rohn (1930-2009)**

Jim Rohn was born in Yakima, Washington and was raised on a farm in Caldwell, Idaho, an only child. A friend invited him to attend a lecture given by entrepreneur Earl Shoaff. In 1955, Rohn joined AbundaVita and became a distributor of the company's product line. Rohn was heavily involved in network marketing in the health supplement industry and became prominent as a speaker and as a business philosopher. He also mentored numerous individuals who had tremendous success, including Mark R. Hughes, the founder of HerbaLife International, and Tony Robbins in the late 1970's. Jim Rohn wrote numerous books and produced many seminars that were recorded with video and/or audio to inspire and encourage others. You can learn more about Jim Rohn at www.jimrohn.com.

Here are some Jim Rohn quotes:

"If you don't design your own life plan, chances are you'll fall into someone else's plan. And guess what they have planned for you? Not much."

"Formal education will make you a living; self-education will make you a fortune."

"Learning is the beginning of wealth. Learning is the beginning of health. Learning is the beginning of spirituality. Searching and learning is where the miracle process all begins."

"If you go to work on your goals, your goals will go to work on you. If you go to work on your plan, your plan will go to work on you. Whatever good things we build end up building us."

8. **Wallace Wattles (1860-1911)**

Wallace Wattles was born and raised in the mid-west in later life. He often travelled to Chicago to lecture on his ideas. He studied the writings of Hegel and Emerson and encouraged others to do the same. He encouraged his readers to test his theories themselves and not just take his word for it. He also practiced the technique of creative visualization. He completed his book *The Science of Getting Rich*, part of a trilogy, in 1910 near the end of his life.

Here are some quotes from Wallace Wattles:

"The very best thing you can do for the whole world is to make the most of yourself."

"Give every person more in use value than you take from them in cash value; then you are adding to the life of the world by every business transaction."

"The grateful mind is constantly fixed upon the best. Therefore, it tends to become the best. It takes the form or character of the best, and will receive the best."

"By thought, the thing you want is brought to you. By action, you receive it."

We are literally surrounded by great people, great ideas and great opportunities on all sides. It is up to us to activate our inner GPS resources to become aware of our own great potential and to become much more aware of the greatness we can tap into to improve and expand our lives each and every day on our journey to becoming a GPS Millionaire! This is also the Secret of the Ages for the 21st Century!

You can do anything you think you can. This knowledge is literally the gift of the gods, for through it you can solve every human problem. It should make of you an incurable optimist. It is the open door.

Robert Collier

Chapter Eleven

Growth Principle – Gratitude

Your responsibility is to think, speak, act the true inner self. Your privilege is to show forth in this self, the fullness of peace and plenty. Keep steadfastly in mind the idea of yourself that you want to see realized. Your daily, hourly, and continual idea of yourself, your life, your affairs, your world and your associates, determines the harvest showing forth. Look steadfastly to your highest ideal of self, and your steadfast and lofty ideal will draw forth blessing and prosperity not only upon you, but upon all who know you. For mind is the only creator, and thought is the only energy.

Robert Collier

I often ask audiences, "When is less more?"

Less is more the moment you realize, with a deep and profound gratitude, that your potential is not limited; it is limitless! When you recognize that an experience, a moment, a profound awareness is not without value; it is, in fact, priceless! No one could possibly put a monetary value on it for you that made any sense whatsoever. ...and even if they tried to do this, you would believe it did not reflect the true value as you understand it, because it is without price – priceless!

If this kind of thinking has not been a priority in your life, or you have falsely minimized the value of these kinds of moments, you need to change your thinking right now. Because it is just this one thing, like the singularity that created the Big Bang, that gave us the universe.

The answer: Less is more when you start to realize that the most important things in life are worth a lot more than money: your life, your family, your health, your relationships, your marvelous mind. When you have truly connected with your inner GPS, this one little point at your center, you begin to understand and grow that concept of less is more – and your life changes dramatically for the better.

The whole process of mental adjustment and atunement can be summed up in one word: gratitude.

Wallace Wattles

You cannot have a GPS Millionaire mindset without gratitude – the one is impossible without the other.

As children, we are told to be grateful for what we have, but that belief, while important, does not have any deep meaning for us as children. It is only when your mature or core thoughts are formed and you are on your own that you realize the sacrifices others have made to help you to get where you are. You begin to realize that they have given you far more than you could ever begin to repay them, for that is when you experience the feeling of deep emotion and of true gratitude for the very first time.

While this initial feeling resonates deeply and is heartfelt, this feeling of gratitude is still in its early stages. You do not yet have the depth and fullness of feeling and the nuance of emotion to be truly grateful for all these things. This realization of gratitude is a profound learning – without deep emotional experience, the true feelings of gratitude that could move you forward will not be there.

How deep have you gone into your self? This was, if you remember, the first step on the way to realizing your GPS Millionaire.

Our friend Bob Proctor says:

Developing a deep and abiding sense of gratitude that is separate from any circumstance or situation is the only way that you will attract wealth. ... It encompasses everything that you might experience – good or bad. When you have a deep and emotional sense of gratitude, you'll perceive every event as an opportunity for growth, and this will enhance your ability to attract wealth. This type of activity is not a temporary activity. It becomes embedded in your sub-conscious; it's a part of who you are, and how you function.

When you put your happiness in a place that is dependent on circumstances – your business, your income, your possessions, etc. – you are living a life of relying on others and the material and impermanent things of life. When you center your feelings of gratitude on the permanent and the ever-present, you are changing yourself. What is permanent and ever-present? Your self and all that has gone into shaping it. What you see as permanent and ever-present becomes accessible to you to use in your life! You must practice every day to develop your gratitude in a deeper and more meaningful way.

Just today, as I picked up my mail, I was reminded of how grateful I am for friends around the world. My friend, Pisey Leng, from New Zealand sent me an autographed copy of her amazing book, *The Wisdom Seeker*. I met Pisey a few years ago in Los Angeles at an event we were attending sponsored by Bob Proctor. It was a small group gathering and we all shared what we were working on at that time. I was working on my first book – GPS Wealth. She explained to us what she was writing about, her book idea and the book title – *The Wisdom Seeker*. I think we all oooh'd and ahhh'd at that title. Pisey and I had several great conversations that week and I remember her telling me that she loved the GPS concept and she saw my book as a great success around the world. I shared with Pisey Leng that I loved her title and the incredible story she was going to share with the world and that everyone would want a copy of her book!! I remember also thinking: I wish I had thought of her book title – *The Wisdom Seeker*. But I didn't. Pisey Leng thought of it – she is an amazing person, it is a brilliant title and a moving and inspiring book that I highly recommend to you. You can buy a copy at www.thewisdomseeker.com – you don't want to miss this one!

Here's an excerpt from the Preface:

Surviving the killing fields is only part of my story. Like millions of Cambodians forced from my home in Phnom Penh into the countryside, I suffered like all so-called newcomers. My dad was executed, and my mom was nearly executed as a result of treachery in a story I will share with you in this book. My brother and I suffered from starvation and infections that left us scarred both mentally and physically. All the newcomers were terrorized and tortured, and we came very close to dying from exhaustion from the long hours of forced labor. I experienced grueling living conditions where our family was forced to live in a tiny hut with another family from another city. There were no sanitary facilities, and we endured constant fear of punishment or death. This was during the best of times for my family living under the Khmer Rouge. I witnessed many horrific and gruesome events that I cannot erase from my memory, despite my best efforts.

Pisey Leng, The Wisdom Seeker

Despite this story of incredible torture, pain and suffering for her family, Pisey Leng has written a book of hope and inspiration for everyone – it is an incredible book. Pisey Leng is truly The Wisdom Seeker!

Why am I sharing this with you? Pisey Leng, in addition to being a beautiful person, is also a lady who demonstrates and shares immense gratitude. In fact, one of the chapters of her book is called *Gratitude, Faith and Persistence*. She writes "I am also very grateful for every experience in my life. People often misunderstand this and ask how can I possibly be grateful for the tragedy that surrounds Cambodia and look at me as if I've lost my marbles. I explain that I cannot change the past, so I choose to let it go and forgive."

WOW! Pisey Leng is a hero as far as I am concerned. She has taken her stand and she is choosing to move forward in her life in a way that demonstrates and commands our utmost respect. Not only is she *The Wisdom Seeker* she is living the principles of a GPS Millionaire. Pisey has truly found the *Secret of the Ages for the 21st Century*.

I was thrilled to receive an autographed copy of *The Wisdom Seeker*. She wrote: "Dear Bruce – It's such a blessing to have met you and to learn from you. Nothing happens by accident, you know that. Thank you for your knowledge and wisdom. Much love and gratitude, Pisey."

I responded with deep appreciation with this note of thanks - "Pisey – I am in awe of your wisdom, talents, abilities and choices for a healthy life and completely humbled by your story. It is my *privilege* and very great honor to be your friend. Thank you, and much love and gratitude to you! - Bruce."

Be grateful for what you have already received, and be grateful for the rich bounty that is on its way.

Pisey Leng, The Wisdom Seeker

When you view the world through the lens of entitlement it often seems that we live in a world of individuals fighting for and defending their rights. They will argue (and argue) that those entitlements MUST be defended at all costs. Anyone who dares to challenge them about it is the enemy and MUST be defeated! It means war to most of us when our entitlements are challenged. I think you can see that this is definitely a competitive issue – little cooperation will be seen around this discussion as it unfolds. In fact, it is more likely to invoke conflict and aggressive behaviors. People don't resist change; they resist being changed.

Why is it that we become disabled into considering that the idea we might be asked to give up could make way for an even better idea or way to live? Is it fear? Is it ego? Is it a closed mind? I think this example also demonstrates that it is virtually impossible to think creatively or openly when you are embroiled in this kind of no-win argument. A closed mind does NOT inspire solution-oriented thinking or problem-solving of any kind. It's basically my way or the highway.

This is the kind of thinking that I grew up with in my family. It was a recipe for conflict and chaos in my early life. I discovered, thankfully, many years ago that this was NOT a successful way to live. For some reason I decided that I was really here as a steward – to perform acts of stewardship. That I would hold roles in my career and at some point would be asked to pass that role on to someone else. This thinking made me proud to be a steward and a giver to and for others– I became an unconscious competent and did not become attached to entitlements.

I began to see life, my life in particular, as a tremendous gift. It is a gift that continued to amaze me the more that I considered how fortunate I was to have it. I began to feel grateful for everything in my life. I must admit that it took me longer to consider being grateful for the bad things, but as I developed this deep feeling of gratitude, my life began to shift – slowly at first, then in a big way.

Gratitude enhances and uplifts. It sends out and transmits a life-giving and life-sharing force that everyone understands and responds to. Gratitude creates space in your mind for more love and more gratitude – because the two are linked. There are many ways to show your gratitude: by speaking it, by demonstrating it, by giving something away to express it, to forgive, to let things go, to stop judging others, to give yourself the gift of gratitude. Be grateful for what you already have! Celebrate your success right now. You might not like what you have, you may want to change it, but you must celebrate what you have already achieved in your life in spite of everything you've faced. Do not condemn what you already have. You want to celebrate it, feel grateful for it and feel and see the abundance that is on its way to you even as you are reading this book.

That is the attitude of success, the attitude that will connect you with your inner GPS. Be grateful for everything – even the difficult things in your life. It is through those challenges and difficulties that you have arrived here. Without them, you would not be the person you are now: ready, and equipped with unique potential to press on to your next goal and challenge. Be grateful that you are on your way to becoming a GPS Millionaire. You can expand your life in ways you haven't even thought of, take advantage of opportunities yet unknown that will be presented to you. Then you can enjoy the excitement of knowing that your inner GPS is directing you toward your goals each and every day. Be deeply grateful for this piece of timeless GPS Wisdom.

If you have begun to realize that there is a power within you, if you have begun to arouse in your conscious mind the ambition and desire to use this power — you have started in the pathway of Wisdom. If you are willing to go forward, to endure the mental discipline of mastering this method, nothing in the world can hinder you or keep you from overcoming every obstacle.

Robert Collier

Chapter 12

Grow Powerful Self

Remember this: The Universal Mind is omnipotent. And when the subconscious mind is in tune with the Higher Self, there is no limit to the things that it can do. Given any desire that is in harmony with the Universal Mind, and you have but to hold that desire in your thought with confident and serene faith to attract from the invisible domain the things you need to satisfy it.

Robert Collier

There is a huge difference between wishing for a thing and expecting it to happen. Expectation is one of the keys to success. When you expect good things to happen, they do. How they will happen is not your concern. Sometimes people get completely caught up in "how" the good things will come to them. And if it doesn't happen that way, they discard the experience – are they really so self-important that things must happen their way? As if they can control nature. This is a mighty ego. The true you, your higher GPS self, waits, because you've overcome ego, and lets it happen. Just expect that good things will happen for you and they will. Let go of the "how" and allow Universal Mind to determine the how.

Having a good attitude is also key. Your attitude is the composite of your thoughts, feelings and actions. It is not any one of those, but all of them combined. Developing positive alignment between your thoughts, feelings and actions will ensure that you develop a great attitude focused on what you want, and not focused on what you don't want.

There is a difference between WISHING for a thing and being READY to receive it. No one is ready for a thing, until he believes he can acquire it. The state of mind must be BELIEF, not mere hope or wish. Open-mindedness is essential for belief.

Napoleon Hill

You must believe in yourself and in your plan and take action on a grand scale. You will move forward and your inner GPS or your Higher Self will connect you to your destination for success every time.

But how can we connect with the inner GPS that leads us to our GPS Millionaire when we can't see it or hold it in our hand like a real GPS device or a GPS app on our cell phone? We need a picture, an image that will help us to better understand the true nature of our mind. Well, the truth is that no one has ever seen the mind. Getting a clear picture of the mind helps you to better understand yourself and how to move forward with information that can not only help you understand YOU better, but is also a tremendous benefit that helps you to understand others. We are all unique and different, yet we are all the same.

This is the paradox of life – you are no different than anyone else, yet you are uniquely you and the way you were created is absolutely perfect. You are God's highest form of creation and God does not make any junk!!

To help us get a picture of the mind, Dr. Thurman Fleet from San Antonio, Texas developed a drawing of the mind back in 1934. This idea was developed further by Bob Proctor with his "Stickperson." Now we unveil to you a 21st Century version of Dr. Thurman Fleet's original idea – The GPS Mind Mapper! It's the secret of the ages – are you paying attention?

The GPS Mind Mapper

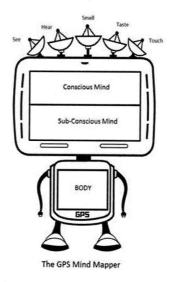

The GPS Mind Mapper

Your conscious mind is your intellectual mind. It is where your logical and reasoning mind is resident – school worked in a small part of this area of the mind.

Your satellite receivers cause you to react to your external world. The Five Senses are – Seeing, Hearing, Smelling, Tasting, Touching. They are like little satellites on the top of our heads.

Your intellectual abilities reside in the conscious mind, you did not learn about this in school at all. Most people are unaware of these factors, but they can be developed. They connect and interact with the silent power of the sub-conscious mind – when used. We all possess these intellectual abilities, but they must be developed.

The six intellectual abilities are: Intuition, Memory, Reason, Will, Perception, and Imagination

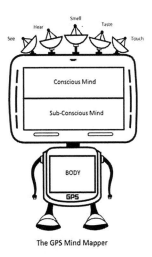

The GPS Mind Mapper

The sub-conscious mind is the most powerful part of your mind. It controls everything in your life – including your growth and the ongoing regeneration of the cells in your body and all your bodily functions. It works 24/7 and never rests. It even is working while you are sleeping. It is so efficient and silently productive that we tend to overlook it but, the truth is, it is like the part of the iceberg you cannot see beneath the waves that is by FAR the largest part.

The sub-conscious mind is where the emotions reside.

The sub-conscious mind also has the ability to connect with your inner GPS (Higher Self) and Universal Intelligence (God) that controls everything. This is the location of your GPS Millionaire. You must act on this information to find it inside yourself.

The GPS Mind Mapper conveys the idea of the mind to the observer. The head is a GPS Tablet screen that is divided in half between the conscious and the sub-conscious minds. When I look at a person, I automatically see a GPS Tablet screen where their head is. Attached to the head are the five satellite receivers – these are receptors for our physical senses that See, Hear, Smell, Taste and Touch. The arms are short little digital (think USB, HDMI and cell phone) connector cables and the body is a small, mini-size GPS Tablet screen and on the feet are the little running shoes – because our GPS Mind Mapper is always on the go in the 21st century.

The information just conveyed to you on the last page is POWERFUL information. Go back and look at it again and THINK. Every person is constructed in this way. Growing your awareness of what causes you to behave leads you to seeing how other people behave as they behave and brings clarity to your mind, allowing you to move forward to all the good things coming into your life with a new-found understanding of your inner GPS. Realize that the more clearly you understand and develop these concepts, the greater will be your success in ALL areas of your life.

It is not how lofty your ambitions are or how much you want things to improve, it's how measurable a difference you are making, living your deepest values and achieving your greatest goals. The GPS Mind Mapper can help you become a GPS Millionaire if you study, apply and develop its wisdom for yourself. Track your progress and pursue your goals with this new information. For it is only when you track progress – one impact point after another – that you mobilize every ounce of your capacity to make the biggest difference in your life, and in the lives of others.

Changing your thinking is difficult, and the brain always seems to figure it can find a way around it. You need to bring all of your intellectual abilities into play in order to override your mind's propensity for repetition, for doing things the same way over and over. You should study the information in this chapter carefully and discipline yourself to learn this new way of thinking about yourself and others. Look within to study and develop your own unique set of intellectual abilities – stretch yourself with these new perceptions. Watch your life dramatically improve and change for the better.

Be the change you want to see in the world.

Think about this statement: "Maybe I should change my mind." When is the last time you heard someone make that statement? Probably not recently. Be the first: stay open, stay heart-centered and connect with your inner GPS and let the ideas flow. And they *will* flow. Faster and faster. It won't be long before you have become a GPS Millionaire!

The proof for you will be in the doing, the taking of action! Testing new ideas and paying attention to their impact on your life is much more important and valuable than listening to us talk about them for you. Only when you do the work and take control will you become inspired to learn even more about yourself – and the world!

You will be empowered with great information to seek growth, prosperity and success with your health, with your relationships and with your finances by aligning with your inner GPS. Then and only then can you share these ideas with others, helping them one person at a time!

Study, Practice, and Teach.
Jim Rohn

There is only one way to connect with your inner GPS and to move forward into your life as a GPS Millionaire, and that is through study. Most people attend seminars and read self-help books and they gather information endlessly. While it is good to have the information, it is useless unless you apply what you are learning to your life. You cannot improve your results just through reading and study alone. You MUST take ACTION!

Make these ideas – the developing of your own inner GPS – the cornerstone of your study program for the next 90 days and watch your results soar out of sight. When you begin to look inside you realize that there is so much more to learn, so much more to do, so much more to give to others, so much more increase in life that you can share than you are doing today. Make it your goal to be one of the energized souls on our planet who is moving forward always seeking more growth, always seeking more prosperity and always seeking more success. You will be amazed at the incredible journey you have begun and you will see how you can go further than you ever imagined you could. Expect it! Claim it! – Take action on the knowledge you have learned in this chapter and all the preceding chapters to Grow your Powerful Self on your journey as a GPS Millionaire!!

The mind is usually thought of as consciousness; but the conscious part of your mind is in fact the very smallest part of it. Ninety percent of your mental life is subconscious, so when you make active use of only the conscious part of your mind you are using but a fraction of your real ability; you are running on low gear. And the reason why more people do not achieve success in life is because so many of them are content to run on low gear all their lives – on SURFACE ENERGY. If these same people would only throw into the fight the resistless force of their subconscious and superconscious (Universal Intelligence) minds, they would be amazed at their undreamed-of capacity for winning success.

Robert Collier

Chapter Thirteen

Growth Principle – Spirituality

Devote your efforts to attaining the realization that the Mind within is the source of true growth, and that the outer expansion of your prosperity will keep exact pace with the spiritual development that takes place within.

Robert Collier

You do not *have* a spirit – you *are* spirit. You inhabit a physical body. Your body is the physical form you have grown from birth and live in every day. That form, which you have created, is moving under your control in and around planet earth – even right now wherever you are as you read this book.

You know that when someone passes on, their form (body) remains behind. We often attend funerals at funeral homes and places of worship where the open casket demonstrates this truth. However, the spirit, the essence of that person is gone, although their physical form remains behind for all to see. Where did their spirit go? This, of course, is an eternal question and the subject of many different beliefs in the religions of the world. No one really knows, although there are certainly books about 'near-death' experiences describing the sensations of the mind that experienced them and what those ideas mean to the person that experienced them.

But it remains an eternal question – for example, the caterpillar morphs into the butterfly. Does the caterpillar know it will become a butterfly? Does the butterfly have any sense that it used to be an earth-bound creature that could not fly at all? There are examples in nature that can give us clues or ideas as to what really happens when you pass on. However, all of it amounts to much speculation.

What we *do* know is that energy is never destroyed. It *cannot* be. Matter and energy are interchangeable. So, the end of your physical presence on earth does not mean your spirit has been destroyed. It is reassuring to think there is some kind of transition that will move our spirit to a higher order of grace and power. Whatever the truth is about passing on, it is not really our concern in this life.

Our concern in this life is about seeking growth, prosperity and success for ourselves in a way that creates the best possible life that we are capable of leading on this earth. That includes becoming more attuned to our own desires through mind and spirit. Most people believe that they are physical beings and occasionally they have a spiritual experience, usually when they are not expecting it. This is not true! We are spiritual beings and we are here on earth having a physical experience. Spirit is always here. Most people are unaware of this. But as we discuss this important GPS Growth Principle, it is vital to become aware of your spirit. Is it familiar to you? ...perhaps a philosopher from the past? ...or a pragmatist? ...or a muse? Remember that nudge the other day telling you, you ought to do "that thing?" Yes. This is your spirit. Your guide.

Dr. Joseph Murphy described it this way in his book *The Power of Your Subconscious Mind* (1961):

Wisdom is the awareness of the tremendous spiritual powers in your subconscious mind and the knowledge of how to apply these powers to lead a full and happy life.

Your goal in life should be to seek **G**reater **P**sychological and **S**piritual awareness, to connect with your inner GPS and to use that information to grow, expand and improve your life on your way to becoming a GPS Millionaire.

Learn to develop and use your intellectual factors that are at the core of your spiritual being: Intuition, Memory, Reason, Will, Perception and Imagination. While every person has the capacity to develop these intellectual factors, not everyone does. Why?

We aren't really taught about them in school, so they are not really very well understood. It is, however, through the use and development of these factors that every famous person who has ever lived has accessed the skills and abilities necessary to grow great fortunes or a tremendous political followings, or lead the field in their particular career area. Without learning about and working on these factors, you will not be able to progress and make connections with your inner GPS or Higher Self. They are essential to that process as well.

Intuition

Your ability to sense the energy around a person or a situation that causes you to feel good about what you are doing and the activities you are involved in or causes you to see "red flags" about a person or a situation: this is Intuition. A reason not to get too close to the person or situation is that your intuition around their energy (negative) or their actions (lacking in thought), or both, causes you to feel uncomfortable while you are working with them. Many people do not act on those feelings and later discover that they should have. The person takes people for a financial ride or they tell false tales to other important business associates in the same careless manner.

Not connecting with or responding to your intuition can lead to terrible consequences. Your intuition generates feelings that speak to you – listen to your intuition and respond faithfully to it. Like those people who listened to an inner voice that told them not to take that airplane. They didn't take the plane and thus saved their lives.

You can't get started until you know what you want. So, if you are not sure then I urge you to trust your intuition. Listen to your intuition and it will tell you.

Dr. Robert Anthony

Memory

People are often told by parents or relatives, "You have a bad memory." This is just not true, for your brain never forgets. You have a perfect memory, but it requires use and practice to make it more effective and efficient in order to unlock it. Some people get quite emotional about their inability to remember things. That's a waste of energy! You must learn to recognize those times as opportunities to practice your perfect memory to improve it so that you don't feel lacking in self-assurance the next time you feel 'put on the spot!' Don't use those moments to put yourself down or to berate yourself for not knowing something "you should have known!" Let it go. Repeat after me: "I have a perfect memory. It just needs to be exercised more."

Reason

Your Reasoning factor is a powerful part of your logical mind. It gives you the ability to think through issues and to make your choices. Are your choices moving you closer to what you want or further away from what you want? Your reasoning factor has, on a daily basis over the course of your life, helped produce results that have either improved your life or made it worse. When your reasoning is faulty your days are not successful, you do not feel good about yourself and your plans and dreams move in a negative direction. When your reasoning is sound and healthy you make good choices, you feel good about yourself and your life seems blessed as you move forward from success to success with great ease. If you are not achieving great success in your life right now, you must look to making better life choices by using your reasoning factor.

Will

Your Will is a very misunderstood intellectual factor. Many people think that they can overcome addictions and faulty behavior by exhibiting a greater will power. Unfortunately, this is not so. Many people think they can use their will on other people to cause them to do, be or gain what they want. Forcing others in this way is manipulative and/or abusive. Any time you use your will to force something to happen at all costs, you are heading in the wrong direction. Force negates. Using your will in this way is destined to fail. You must learn to use your will by applying its abilities on yourself in a positive manner so you move towards what you want. In order to connect with your inner GPS, you need only use your will power upon yourself and then watch your GPS Millionaire begin to emerge.

Perception

You must learn to see the underlying truth in all things. You must see beneath all seemingly wrong conditions the great one life ever moving forward toward fuller expression and more complete happiness.
Wallace D. Wattles

Our perceptions shape our lives whether we are aware of them or not. Are you aware of your perceptions? As you think about your world and the issues that you are involved in, you want to be sure that your thinking is informed by positive and open perceptions. Perceptions that inspire, uplift and unfold your life in a direction that takes you to what you want. Your higher self understands that perceptions that stimulate you to do your best cannot fail to bring you success and every good thing in life.

By activating your inner GPS, you are stimulating your perceptions towards your highest good. By setting your sights on goals that excite, challenge and maybe even scare you all at the same time, you create the conditions that take you in a direction far from the masses. Your perception also tells you that your life is moving on to a higher frequency of success!

My late father-in-law, Alan A. Robertson, was a self-made multi-millionaire. He came to Canada from Scotland when he was 18 years old, a high school graduate from Bell Baxter High School in Cupar, Scotland. He worked for many years for Honeywell Inc., retiring with a good pension. However, he wanted more from his life and became a real estate agent, and went into that business following his forced retirement from Honeywell. He also began purchasing homes in the Toronto area that he could rent to families. His business income, assets and financial success all took off – he had found his GPS Millionaire!

I was most fortunate to learn and hear about how he achieved his success directly from him. He was a modest man who came from humble roots. He came to Canada and achieved massive success. If he could do it, you can do it, too!

One of the things that always troubled Alan, during later life, was the death of his own father. His father was an accountant who never seemed to be able to make it happen in his own life. In time, he grew ill and was unable to work the last few years of his life. Of course, Alan loved his father and looked up to him. Alan remembered the day of his father's funeral – a bleak, grey day at a cemetery in Manchester, England where his Dad was buried. Alan was so devastated and distraught at the age of 12, and, to make matters worse, he was not allowed to attend at the gravesite; he remained in the car nearby sobbing while his Dad's body was buried. He told me he remembered the tree near where the car had been parked, but he could not remember the name of the cemetery. He had no idea where the grave was located and his Mother was left in such a poor condition with Alan and his sister to raise, that they could not afford to put a headstone on the grave. Alan's mother passed away many years later, but the grave was left unmarked and remained unmarked for over 50 years. This troubled Alan a great deal because he loved his Dad and looked up to him. It wasn't right.

At that time, 1947, other family members with greater means watched the tragedy unfold and did little to help Alan's mother. In the early 2000's, my wife, Gail and I and his grandson, Cameron, encouraged him to first find the cemetery and the location of the grave so that he could return to England to visit where his Dad was buried. Then, he could make plans to have a stone placed on the grave to honor his father's memory. Alan liked this idea and let it grow inside him. Alan and his wife searched on the Internet for the cemeteries in the area and each one was contacted with a request for information. Sure enough it was soon established exactly which cemetery his Dad was buried in. Alan made plans to visit the grave. We continued to encourage him to prepare the gravestone, so that he could honor his Dad during his visit overseas. Gail searched for a quotation to add to the gravestone.

Alan learned that three other relatives were also buried in the unmarked grave – so their names were added to the stone. Alan loved the Robbie Burns quote that Gail found: "Recollect for what once thou wast." This quotation was added to the stone below the names. Alan ordered the stone and then went overseas to see it laid in place on the grave 60 years after his father's death. All of this was made possible by Alan's intuition and perception – then he took action on those feelings to develop a solution that made him feel SO much better about his own life. He even told me later that he had found the tree he remembered by the grave site. It was a great feeling for him. Alan had healed a huge wound that had been in his life those many years and closed a painful loop in his life that had been left open. It was a great thing – and all the more special for Gail and her family because Alan passed away just 2 years later.

Imagination

Without leaps of imagination or dreaming, we lose the excitement of possibilities. Dreaming, after all is a form of planning.
Gloria Steinem

Live out of your imagination, not your history.
Stephen R. Covey

Your imagination is the key to your creativity. When you were a child, you dreamed and fantasized endlessly. As we have discussed, you learned early in your life as a student that daydreaming was "bad" and you had to stop doing it or your parents would be notified. Basically fear was used to encourage you to stop leaving the reality of the classroom in your mind. Of course, imagination is the key to some of the greatest scientific discoveries and artistic creations the world has ever known. Even if YOU think today that you are NOT creative – I can assure you that you are VERY creative. To stop being creative for you would be akin to consciously choosing to stop breathing – it is effectively impossible to do! In fact, your creative imagination is awe-inspiring.

How do you access this innate creativity? You open the door to your self. You get rid of that teacher voice on your shoulder; you get rid of mom and dad silently telling you it's not practical.

Remove those barriers so the way in is unobstructed and then listen to your spirit.

Carefully read the words of Sir Paul McCartney that follow and think – when he received the Gershwin Prize he said these words humbly, quietly and with humility before performing a song that was voted the Best Song of All Time by *MTV* & *Rolling Stone* in 2000.

This idea of the mystery of it is part of being creative and being a musician. Some of the songs you write, you don't know where they come from. You don't know quite how it happens and there is no amount of training that can really teach you how to do it. You are just lucky when they come. You know it's a very mysterious, magical process as anyone who has written a song knows. The song we are going to do now to finish this evening is a song that came to me in a dream and so I have to believe in the magic. I was very lucky because this tune was in my head and I woke up and put some piano chords to it. I went around for weeks asking my friends, George Martin, our producer, and John Lennon & George Harrison, "What is this song here? It must have come from somewhere? I don't know where it came from." And nobody could place it so in the end I had to kind of claim it as my own. You know, that's pretty....magic. You just wake up one morning and there is this tune in your head and then about over three thousand people go and record it.

Sir Paul McCartney on receiving The Gershwin Prize from the U.S. Congress - June 2, 2010; speaking about his song *Yesterday*.

The purpose of existence is GROWTH. You can't grow spiritually or mentally without happiness. ...Divine ideas in your spiritual consciousness will become active in your business, and will work out as your abundant prosperity.

Robert Collier

Chapter Fourteen

Generous Prosperity Sensibility

You will find in Universal Mind the key to the control of every circumstance, the solution to every problem, the satisfaction of every right desire. But to use that key, you must bear in mind the three requisites of faith in your powers, initiative, and courage to start. ... Without the three requisites, you will never do it.

Robert Collier

It's not how lofty your intentions are or how much you want things to improve; it's the measurable difference you are making in living your deepest values and achieving your greatest goals. Only when you track progress – one impact point at a time after another – do you mobilize every ounce of your capacity to make the biggest difference.

It's not how well you plan your time, it's how effectively you put your attention on what matters most ... in advance and as unexpectedly as it appears. What really matters ignores the clock. The busier you get, the harder it is to see anything except what's right in front of you. So, you may not realize how much you are missing, but it's a lot.

To live an exceptionally rich GPS Millionaire life, you have to be respectful of time while also being attuned and aligned to seizing the right moments, both as you plan for them and, more often, as they appear from out of nowhere. Unless you can learn to let go of marching to the clock, you will continue getting in your own way, missing life and many of your deeper chances to make a difference along the way.

You can be paying so much attention to this one thing you're doing that you're blind to a whole lot of things: This is called intentional blindness. This is one way your mind can misdirect you when it *thinks* it is doing the right things. By the time you notice, it's too late. Better to stay focused and mindful. It's best to avoid mistakes.

People often hang on to old solutions and beliefs that have far outlived their usefulness. Why do people constantly think that repeating old habits that have been unsuccessful, will suddenly become successful? The phrase 'riding a dead horse' comes to mind. Here is a humorous example of how that thinking can be followed to unbelievably poor results – often in a corporate or business setting. Do you recognize anything here? Time to re-evaluate and stop right away!!

What To Do If You Are Riding a Dead Horse – The Top Ten List –

10. Buy a stronger whip
9. Change riders
8. Declare, "This is the way we've always ridden this horse!"
7. Appoint a team to revive the dead horse.
6. Ignore the dead horse…What dead horse?
5. Create a training session to improve your riding skills.
4. Outsource contractors to ride the dead horse.
3. Appoint a committee to study the dead horse.
2. Arrange a visit to other sites to see how they ride dead horses.
1. Harness several dead horses together for increased speed.

The correct answer to the question, according to a Native American saying, is to dismount. But our brain loves to stick with a plan, even when it isn't working, in the belief that sooner or later it must work. The same mentality that makes people play the lottery month after month, day after day, even though the odds of winning are astronomical. Most people say, "You can't win if you don't have a ticket." However, the truth is you are more likely to lose a lot continually if you have purchased a ticket! The odds are extremely high against you. Sometimes people have to be dying to realize that they have been wasting their energy on *not* living when they believe they have been living. Once you have recognized these tendencies in yourself, you can see how you need to change your thinking to foster your *Generous Prosperity Sensitivity*. Your inner GPS can help you move toward what you want. In the final analysis, you can only do this by completely letting go of what you really don't want – and what hasn't yet worked and never will work for you. You're not mid-stream, it's okay to change horses, you won't drown. Once you make a start toward what your deeper self wants, the truth becomes evident that nothing can stop you from achieving your own GPS Millionaire.

> *The secret of getting ahead is getting started.*
> Mark Twain

You must know what you want and be passionate about it to attract it to you, as I've said before. You will NEVER get started if you decide that you must SEE it before you will BELIEVE it. If you won't take a risk before what you want appears, you are going to find it very difficult to grow and change your life. You're really just standing still, like a rat on an exercise wheel. You've got to decide to stop WAITING for things to happen and take ACTION to make things happen, and then the law of attraction will begin to work for you in a positive way.

The law of attraction is the name given to the maxim, "like attracts like." This philosophy is used to sum up the idea that by focusing on positive or negative thoughts a person brings positive or negative experiences and people into their life. Why? Because people and their thoughts are both made from pure energy and like energy attracts like energy.

Thus, the trouble with not achieving is in the mind. We must put a value on mind according to its worth – and it's worth a lot! Therefore, if your mind has been deceived by some invisible enemy into a negative belief, you have put it into the form of a disease to be able to combat it. Only when the disease, your thought enemy, your old baggage, has been driven out can you discover the truth of the law of attraction.

The law of attraction is *always* in operation. It brings to each person the conditions and experiences that they predominantly think bout or which they desire or expect. Yes? So, if you're riding a dead horse, what do you think you're going to get? Right. Nothing and Nowhere.

The law of attraction will certainly and unerringly bring to you the conditions, environment and experiences that will bring you success.

Ralph Waldo Trine wrote, in *In Tune With The Infinite* (1897):

The law of attraction works universally on every plane of action, and attracts whatever we desire or expect. If we desire one thing and expect another, we become like houses divided against themselves, which are quickly brought to desolation. Determine resolutely to expect only what you desire, then you will attract only what you wish for.

We want to learn to use all of our intellectual factors to make this happen; however, use of these factors is limited by our perception of reality. We all have some natural limitations in the way we perceive reality but we are not limited by it unless we CHOOSE to be limited. In order to change this, we must take stock of ourselves and see if our perception of reality needs to change in order to attract something more in focus with what we truly want. Our state of awareness determines the clarity with which we perceive and understand everything that affects us. If our awareness is faulty, our actions will take us in the wrong direction.

Belief in limitation is the one and only thing that causes limitation.
Thomas Troward

The truth is, you must know what you want before you can become aware of the new direction you must follow to bring it into reality. Valuable opportunities and information will come your way when you know exactly what you want. It's the old story: when you buy a particular make and model of a red sports car – suddenly you see that car everywhere on the road. Usually even more of them than you ever noticed previously! What has increased? The actual number of cars? No. Your awareness: you have attracted that awareness to you.

There is simply too much information coming at us constantly; it is impossible for all of it to get through. Determining exactly what you want to see will allow your mind to sort through, in a highly selective way, exactly the information and opportunities that you want to take advantage of and profit from on your journey to becoming a GPS Millionaire. It's a natural and exciting way to grow your Generous Prosperity Sensitivity.

Let us not look back in anger, nor forward in fear, but around us in awareness.

Leland Val Van De Wall

You don't need to know all the answers. In fact, having too much information can work against you – your logical mind mulls over all of those zillions of facts and you become mired in inaction – you have *too many facts* to consider. You become overwhelmed, and inaction is the normal reaction to that feeling. What you need to know is, what you need to focus on is: Where do I want to end up? What will the end result be? What do I want to create? Edgar Alan Poe says this about writing a story – and your life is a story you are writing right now – that you must know where you are going before you begin.

Attract the answers to these questions and all the information necessary to your success will come flooding your way. Your inner GPS, your Higher Self, will begin to move you to your destination in the most efficient and effective manner. But you must program and commit to heading towards your destination, your end result, FIRST!

High Performance action-oriented individuals know that BELIEVING is SEEING. Everyone else wants to gather the facts, check things out, wait for the time to be right, etc. But it doesn't work that way. These become just excuses for inaction. You must BELIEVE in the goal first, then you will see how to create it. Just take the next logical step…but BELIEVE in the end result first and have faith in yourself.

It's important to show willingness. Be willing to think outside your preconceived limitations. Don't think about why you *can't* do something, think about how you *can*. Don't think about why it won't work; think about why it will work. Don't think about "what if it doesn't…," instead think about "What if it does?!?"

This means focusing on the solution rather than the problem. This requires a shift in your paradigm if you have been a problem-solver for most of your life, as many of us have. I was a fixer – people always seemed to want my help and ideas on how to solve problems – but instead of focusing on the solutions, I found myself in my young life always focusing on the problem. I was focusing on the negative as the way to solve what was going on. This never works.

What happened for me at that time was that I learned that I could use my sub-conscious mind to gain answers or create solutions or to come up with reasons and excuses why the problem couldn't be solved. I was not open and I did not allow the opportunity to present itself that would move things forward in a positive way. The choice is always there for all of us: to observe a situation and stay open, to keep our heart open and to listen to our inner GPS for directions on what to do next. The choice always remains yours to make – are you making positive choices? Always remember – focus your GPS Millionaire Mind in one direction toward what you want in order to be effective, stay open and keep it positive!!

No one ever did a good piece of work while in a negative frame of mind. Your best work is always done when you are feeling happy and optimistic.

Robert Collier

My problem in those early days of my life was rooted in low self-esteem. I learned that since we can only attract that which we feel worthy of, the greater your feelings of self-esteem the higher the value you have in yourself, the more you see yourself as a person with options and show less concern about risk. You also are seen as a more open person by others and they will be attracted to you – as a customer, client or friend.

You have to become a better student and allow others to be your teachers. Some can show you a better way, if you are open to receive it. Some can teach you by their mistakes. Some can share their wisdom, enthusiasm and experiences to improve your bottom line. If they can show you how to get where you want to go easier, better and faster ask yourself – Why am I holding myself back? Why am I getting in my own way? Say instead, "No! I want to become better. Say, "I want to learn more about becoming a GPS Millionaire!" Then take action and follow through to do it!

Once you have decided what you want, how you want to live, what you personally want to create, the excitement builds because the information will come through and you will take action and see a way to make it happen!

When you have a great idea or belief and you are seeking to create something that did not exist before: a new service, or a new product or business. Your difficulty won't be your belief in the idea, product or service. It will be trying to convince others in your circle that it is possible. The challenge is getting those people to BELIEVE in YOU!

See the things you want as already yours. Know that they will come to you at need. Then LET them come. Don't fret and worry about them.... Think of them as YOURS, as belonging to you, as already in your possession.

Robert Collier

Be extremely careful when selecting the kind of people with whom you surround yourself, because they strongly influence your creativity whether you are aware of it or not. Negativity can become contagious in an office setting, in relationships, in your family and your business. People who believe that things can't be done want to prove themselves right. However, people who KNOW things can be done go out and MAKE IT HAPPEN! Surround yourself with people of high self-esteem who can tell you how to get the job done, how to make it happen! Attract the right kinds of people to support you in developing your idea, your new product, your business or your relationships. You can only do this if your mind is in the right attitude.

You must have FAITH that you can attract the people, resources and energy that will take you where you want to go.

You must believe in the POWER of something invisible – FAITH. I don't mean faith in the religious sense. When you understand that it is your FAITH or belief in your ability to create (NOT compete) that determines your results, you are then empowered to go forward and accomplish tasks that the most people would consider impossible!

Activate your inner GPS by attracting the kinds of energized, enthused and positive-thinking people to your team that are seeking to support great ideas and actions. Give them inspiration and encouragement to fulfill their dreams and support them as they move forward in their own lives. The more you give them, the more you will receive yourself – it becomes an upward spiral of success attracting wonderful new ideas and experiences, but also improved business, improved customer relations, improved family relationships, improved finances – and a **Generous Prosperity Sensitivity**. There is nothing better than seeing the application of these GPS Millionaire principles generating wealth in so many different areas in your life each and every day and providing great benefit in the lives of others!

Open up your mind. Clear all the channels of thought. Keep yourself in a state of receptivity. Gain a mental attitude in which you are constantly expecting good.

Robert Collier

Chapter Fifteen

Gain Profitable Synergy

Remember that the only limit to your capabilities is the one you place on them. There is no law of limitation. The only law is of supply. Through your subconscious mind you can draw upon universal supply for anything you wish. The ideas of Universal Mind are as countless as the sands on the seashore. Use them. And use them lavishly, just as they are given.

Robert Collier

1. Start Your Own Business

Believe it or not, you *can* start your own business right now, today! This is the best thing that you can do at this moment to take action on these principles. Why? Because it sends a message to your brain that you are NOT an employee. You will NEVER achieve wealth by remaining an obligated employee for your entire working life. Does it shock you to realize that you have spent most of your career making someone else wealthy? If you have worked in any industry (and I would say 96% of us have!)

as an employee, that is precisely what you have been doing. It's because you have been trading your time for money. That is absolutely the worst way to earn money. I am NOT suggesting that you go right now and quit your job. What you should do is start your own business now, even while still employed by someone else. Work at your business in your spare time and build an income stream that matches your employed income. Then, you will be in a position to decide just what should be done to grow your business further at that time.

When looking for a name for your business remember – You can use your name in your business, your street, your neighborhood, the actual product you will be selling, whatever feels best to you to market both yourself and your business to the public. Also, remember to search the availability of websites for the name and reserve the addresses you want. You can develop the online presence later – but get those web addresses reserved you want NOW.

Consider how your business will develop. Is it a bricks and mortar business, a mailbox address that you rent, or is it an online business that you run from your home? Remember, there will be issues when you deal with the public, so consider carefully whether or not you prefer to have customers who know where you live. If you are using phone contact information, cell numbers are to be preferred to home phone numbers, again, for obvious reasons. Do you have a logo for your business? A creative business name? Do you need business cards? There are inexpensive places to get professionally produced business services and materials that can get you started in a great way. Taking the first step activates your inner GPS and moves you toward your GPS Millionaire.

2. Look for Opportunities to Serve Others

Is there a need in your community that is not being filled? My friends Neil & Rachel Oliver in Toronto, Canada looked around their community and started a "rent-to-own" business to connect people interested in investing in real estate who need a little bit of help to get started on their first property with all the details. Check out their website at: www.renting2own.ca.

My friend, Clare Cook, from Hoboken, New Jersey helps Brides and Professionals to live their lives weighing what they want! She does incredible work helping others to live in a healthy and fit manner. She started out with an idea to help Brides prepare for their weddings by weighing what they wanted for their big day. She serves her customers by creating meal plans that are healthy and fun. Check out her website at www.weighwhatyouwant.com Clare has found her inner GPS and is on her journey to towards her GPS Millionaire goals.

Become aware of some of the products and services that are available in your area. What is not available? What kinds of products and services could provide the base for a successful business that are not currently in your area? What products and services are available now in your area that might be offered at a cheaper price, but still generate a healthy profit margin? Sometimes utilizing a skill or ability that you have to provide products or services to others in an efficient, cost-effective manner can put you in front of your customers in a most positive way and create the business vehicle that allows good money to accumulate in your bank account. When you are serving others you create a direct channel to your GPS Millionaire Mind and the idea itself begins to resonate within you and grow inside – and out.

3. Build Multiple Sources of Income (MSIs)

Your goal should always be to create multiple sources of income – this is NOT another job, but rather income that is derived from different sources – some big, some small but all combining to bring the flow of dollars into your bank. There are many ways to multiply your effectiveness by becoming involved in generating positive cash flow. Some examples include creating a "how-to" video to sell to others, an audio or MP3 or CD recording, or an online seminar or program available for purchase. There are many, many ways to create something that you can sell that is available to others for purchase online 24/7. This is an MSI – you can earn money with it, because you developed it and sold it. It has the potential to remain an income stream even later when you are doing other things with your life. You can even be making money globally while you are asleep, selling your ideas, products or services on the internet.

This is a concept that absolutely confounded me when I first heard it. The truth is that most of us have learned through our parents or our schooling that you earn money by trading your time for it – you do a job and you make a stipulated amount per hour. This is absolutely the worst way to earn money and has been the cause holding so many people back for their entire lives. Why is this? The main reason is because it creates individuals who think like employees – they're not as good as the bosses, they can't do any better – rather than realizing that they are working for themselves. Each person's potential to earn money is unlimited. However, people put a self-imposed limitation on themselves by believing that an hourly rate is all that they are entitled to earn and all that they can achieve. It is a self-deception that causes them to stop looking for other ways to increase their earning power.

We should always be looking for the BEST way to create and develop as many MSIs as possible in our life in order to maximize our earning potential and to keep the money flowing into and through our lives. This idea also invokes a law – the law of circulation: once the money begins to flow, it flows in ever-increasing quantities like water flowing downhill. Use your imagination and apply your creativity to this idea and watch your earning power and income increase. You are connected in a BIG way to your inner GPS, your Higher Self, when you begin to fully understand the concept of MSIs and TAKE ACTION on it!!

4. Develop a Business Website and Facebook Page

Marketing your idea, product or service is an important step in getting the word out to others that you have something amazing and unique to provide to the world. One of the most effective ways to get the word out is to develop a website for your business that spells out what you can do.

Most people think that they must possess the necessary skills themselves to produce and maintain a website on the internet. Then they get bogged down in deciding (or not) that they must acquire the skills necessary to create the website, do the graphics, write the copy, etc. There are outstanding professionals who are available to help you at very reasonable cost, if you will take advantage of their talents and services. This, of course, involves some team-building, but you can make arrangements with them to develop the kind of website that will grow your business. Usually, they can also recommend the kind of presence your business needs to have on Social Media – primarily Facebook – but there are others you should investigate including Twitter, Instagram, etc., that may help to boost the visibility of your business.

If you are ready to learn more, read my friend Mike Schryer's book – *The Facebook Phenomenon – How to Leverage Your Social Network to Grow Your Business*. You can visit Mike Schryer and his partner Jennifer and take advantage of their fantastic programs that will lead you to success in your marketing on Facebook at www.iinspireinc.com.

Although you are paying developers on a fee-for-service basis, they actually become part of your team and will give you advice and suggestions on how best to proceed to get your message out to the marketplace. You should stay open to their suggestions and ideas because their support will help you to move your business forward on the internet, but ultimately all the final decisions are yours to make and it is important that you make those decisions with an eye on Growth, Prosperity and Success (GPS) for you and your business!

Suddenly with a business website you are now able to provide your services around the world. This is a surprising thought to most people. I remember how excited I was when I made book sales from my business website in New Zealand and Sweden one night while I was sleeping!! Your satellite in the sky is turned on 24/7 and your GPS Millionaire can be bringing business from all over the globe right to YOUR door and into your bank account!!

5. Write a Book

A book can be a great MSI. Once you have completed your book it has the potential to become a tremendous business and marketing tool. It can even become the basis for your business if you like writing and want to write more books. The fact is you can have a book that is a physical book, an eBook or an audio or video book, or all of the above. The choice is yours today as to which format you wish to create. Just take your area of expertise or interest and begin to map out what your book would look like.

Do you have an idea for a book? Do you have a title? My co-author, Raymond Aaron, is an expert at helping people bring their book to the marketplace. Go to www.aaron.com for more great information on his 10-10-10 Program!

When you write your book it becomes your calling card or brand. It speaks about you in a larger way than just giving a speech or a talk to others. You also become a part of the much smaller percentage of people in the world who have written a book. Most people in the world have NOT written a book, so you have stepped beyond that group by making the decision to write your own book. Once your book is complete, it remains a continuing source of business growth and development for you. Why? Because it is your book, you wrote it. You can continue to use it in helping others with your ideas for the rest of your life – which can be quite a long time. Then, after you are gone, your family and heirs can continue to control the financial benefits of your authorship for a significant period of time.

There are many tremendous business benefits for writing a book. My advice to you is – go for it and write the book! Words have great power and they move people in all sorts of ways – positively and negatively. When you apply your creativity to this truth and begin writing, sending out positive and uplifting messages to a world in need of inspiration and hope for the future, you are making a huge difference in the world. You become much more aware that the earth vibrates and is moving. Your book helps you to connect with your GPS Millionaire Mind that is there waiting to guide you forward towards a more exciting Growth, Prosperity and Success!

6. Network and Support Other Like-Minded Entrepreneurs

There are many ways that people can come together who think in a similar way to promote and support their business endeavors in a cooperative and creative manner. You may not feel that you know a lot of people who support your ideas. There is only one way to discover this and move forward, and that is through networking. You must attend seminars, live or online, and gather information about who is interested in the kinds of ideas, products and services that you are interested in. Share your ideas with others and you will be amazed at the number of people who want to share their ideas with you.

Don't forget that you are doing this to be cooperative and NOT competitive. The minute you begin to feel your competitive spirit entering the discussion, you are in trouble in this kind of environment. Instead, offer to give whatever is needed in order to keep the flow of ideas and information flooding towards you as well as others. You want the best of Growth, Prosperity and Success (GPS) for EVERYONE – not just yourself.

Your business itself can be developed through network marketing. There are great opportunities in this industry for you to develop and grow your own business. The added bonus is that as you develop your business you will meet individuals who are also seeking to expand and grow their businesses and you will have the opportunity to learn through networking with them. This will expand your knowledge and understanding of entrepreneurship and help you in a practical way with ideas and information to grow your business. Your inner roadmap, your inner GPS, knows that this environment is the best possible place for you to be to soak in some amazing energy, to tap into ideas, products and services that present you with great opportunities for massive growth and greatly increased profitability in your life and your business.

7. Develop Video and/or Audio Programs

This may seem, at first glance, like an absurd idea to you right now. You may think, "They say that speaking in public is one of the most stressful things a person can do! So now, you are asking me to actually talk intelligently while I am being recorded on video? Are you crazy? No!"

I am putting the idea in your head that you *do* have the ability and potential to share the thoughts of your marvelous mind with others in a positive manner. One way to do this that can increase your business is through developing a program that teaches ideas that hold value to others. This is being of great service to provide information that people need to know. Also, you can practice – you don't have to be great the first time you do anything; you just have to make an effort to do it over and over again. You learned to ride a bicycle when you were a youngster. You had never been on a bike successfully before that. You graduated from your tricycle to your bicycle. Sometimes the transition involved several days of bumps and bruises – but then the day came when you just glided through the air on your bike and you have never looked back! The truth is, the more you practice something the better you will get at it. When you ride your bike today, you don't think at all about those bumps and bruises you picked up years ago when you were learning to ride, do you?

That is powerful knowledge – know that there will be bumps and bruises as you develop your video/audio programs, but forget it and keep focusing on trying to get better at it. … and YOU WILL! A video and/or audio program can be a fantastic way to grow your business and provide information to the public about the ideas, products or services you are seeking to inform them about. It also connects them with you and your wonderful positive energy. Always consider how these tremendous tools can assist you in growing your business and GPS Millionaire Mind that will guide you in just the right way to find the best road to travel to your amazing success.

8. Build your email list

Take action to build your email list. This should be a definite priority since having an email list that contains the addresses of people who are interested in the things you are selling is the keys to the kingdom. What do I mean? Well – many businesses spend a lot of time trying to FIND the people who are interested in what they are selling. This involves the use of a lot of money and resources and sometimes a great deal of time to simply get the message to those who want to receive it. When you realize that your message is going out to a lot of people who are NOT ready to receive it, it can be discouraging. However, here is the shift – ONLY the people who want to hear from you and are interested in what you are selling are on your email list to begin with. You have SAVED all of those resources that were wasted in searching for those people, by building an email list of like-minded people. This completely guarantees your success! Why? Because you are reaching out each time you use your list to those who are eager to receive what you are sending them. You can NOT be successful sending your messages out to those who are NOT interested in reading, seeing or hearing them!! So begin to think of ways that you can build your email list.

What are some of the ways? You can ask people for their email address, you can purchase someone else's list, you can obtain their email address on your website, and you can give them a gift in return for their email address. There are also email list professionals who can help you to build your list for a fee. There are many ways to do it – just begin thinking about all the different ways you can acquire email addresses from those who WANT your information and you will be well on your way to success and your inner GPS for Wealth will be activated and vibrating on a MUCH higher frequency.

I built my email list by using a free product I developed called – Your GPS Daily Directions! It's a free email service delivering a piece of GPS Wisdom to your email inbox every business day. You can sign up for it right now by going to my website – www.gpsmillionaire.com

9. Do it NOW!!

If you found yourself reading the previous eight examples and the little voice in your mind was saying why you couldn't do this or that – STOP! These are rationalizations trying to stop you dead in your tracks. They are success-killers that have likely held you back for years and years. It is time now to break that paradigm!

Go back to the beginning of the chapter and read it through again. This time, though, I want you to think of at least three ways in each category of how you CAN do it. Procrastination is one of the scourges of our age – it is time to stop it and get into action mode. Don't think at all about why you can't do it. ONLY think of ways that you can! Put down your remote, get off the sofa – let's do it right now. Move out of your comfort zone and take a risk to make it happen! Suddenly, the people and resources that you need will appear in your life, because you are focusing on a positive outcome for your desires.

You will be shocked and delighted at how much better you will feel when you begin to see the idea, product or service that you visualized in your mind coming closer into reality with each passing day as you take ACTION on these ideas. You have the potential, the ability and the talent to be a more effective person and to create these exciting conditions in YOUR FUTURE – but that amounts to nothing if you don't do it now! Doing it NOW hard-wires you to your inner GPS, your Higher Self and moves you like a rocket away from the masses and into AMAZING Growth, Prosperity and Success (GPS) levels. Do it NOW!

Decide now what you want of life, exactly what you wish your future to be. Plan it out in detail. Vision it from start to finish. See yourself as you are now, doing those things you have always wanted to do.

Make them REAL in your mind's eye – feel them, live them, believe them, especially at the moment of going to sleep, when it is easiest to reach your subconscious mind – and you will soon be seeing them in real life.

The time to begin is NOW. It is never too late.

Robert Collier

Chapter Sixteen

Gain or Pain Solutions

All riches have their origin in Mind. Wealth is an idea – not money. Money is merely the material medium of exchange for ideas. The paper money in your pockets is in itself worth no more than so many pieces of paper. It is the idea behind it that gives it value....So don't go out seeking wealth. Look within you for ideas!

Robert Collier

If you are the type of person that has to do things their way or not at all – I have a question for you: Why don't you have what you want yet?

If you are the kind of person that believes that you know and understand the way to success and wealth – I have a question for you: Why aren't you wealthy and successful yet?

If you believe that the only person you can have a lifelong, happy relationship with must meet your standards – I have a question for you: Why are you not yet in a lifelong, happy relationship yet?

I am not trying to be mean. There is a reason I am asking uncomfortable questions for many of you. There is a reason you are reading this book. It is because you don't know something. For years you have been going to people for advice who also did not know. You thought they knew, but they didn't. They couldn't help you, but for some reason you sought out their advice – you kept doing so until you then decided that their advice wouldn't work, so you kept doing what you wanted to do, what you thought might work, even though it was not working for you. You now know it could never have worked for you or anyone else. Why do you do this? So, you see, I am not trying to be mean.

Sometimes there is comfort in the routine and habit of continuing to do what we know won't work. Others call it insanity. You probably have been gathering this kind of self-help information for some time now – maybe even for years. Continuing to gather information will not do it for you either. You have to ACT on the information you get from people who KNOW how to help you get there.

Raymond Aaron and I know how to get what we want. We are both wealthy, successful and in happy and healthy relationships. We know what we are talking about. We can help you get there, too!

Are you willing to take action?

Your answer to that question will determine whether or not the results in your life become a gain or a pain solution. Which is it going to be for you?

What do I mean by gain or pain? Well, think about it for a moment. Most of the solutions we come up with in our lives produce either gain or pain, though there are some solutions that are neutral. If the decisions you are making in your life are producing more PAIN than GAIN let me tell you – you are doing it WRONG!!

Isn't it about time that you recognized that you can't get there without help? The truth is you cannot do it alone. Never can, never will. The fact is, after all, that no one does. Everyone needs help along the way in pursuit of their goals and dreams. When you recognize the importance of this in your own life, you have taken the first step. You must allow and be willing to receive the information you need from the people that can help you achieve your dreams.

You have to get on a path that will lead you to your GPS Millionaire that helps you study and develop ideas about:

1. Your GPS Inner Resources – the amazing things you can do to find your 'second wind' & keep the creative juices flowing.
2. Our Natural Resources – the bounty that the earth provides for all of us in abundance
3. GPS Mindstorming – How 30 minutes with a sheet of paper can dazzle you into your future!!
4. Charting Your Life to Achieve GPS! – Where are you now? Where are you going? What's available now? What remains? How can you maximize your effectiveness?
5. Joining The GPS Club! – How would you like to have access to a phenomenal group of Minds around the world? Become part of a Mastermind movement that will blow your mind!!

Following these five Growth, Prosperity and Success points will make your GPS Millionaire a reality that results from setting your sights directly on what you want. This process not only ensures your success, it guarantees it. The added benefit to it is the person you must become in order to have it. There is no more of winning deals at someone else's expense. You are not in competition or conflict with anyone else. You are constantly working on becoming a better person yourself. That is the secret.

The truth is that in order to have more, you have to become more than you are right now. You become more by focusing on doing your best each and every day – being a better you than you were yesterday. Measure your results constantly to see that you are moving each day closer to your goal and not farther away. These are the gain or pain solutions referred to in the chapter title – if you are moving further away from your goal, there is pain. When you move closer to your goal, there is gain. That is how the system works and you are the cause, you are the decision-maker who makes it all happen.

Following these five steps is crucial to your **G**rowth, **P**rosperity and **S**uccess. It is a new way to unleash the power of your mind to take you where you want it to go in an easy, stress-free manner, choosing the steps each day, each moment that will get you there. There will be days when you feel the pain, but if your days of success outweigh your days of failure then you must inevitably reach your destination, and Growth, Prosperity and Success will become a way of life for you.

The choice is yours to make. Make the right choice.

1. Inner Resources – Finding Your 'Second Wind'

Open the channels between your mind and Universal Mind, and there is no limit to the riches that will come pouring in. Concentrate your thoughts on the particular thing you are most interested in, and ideas in abundance will come flooding down, opening a dozen ways of winning the goal you are striving for.

Robert Collier

Begin to think in a new way – think about your results and measure your progress towards what you want. Use your passion and persistence to keep your eye on the goal you have set for yourself. These are your inner energy resources that can create tremendous abundance in your life. Focus them and use them for your benefit. Realize that the future is of your making. You are the only power that can prevent you from achieving your goals. Forget the obstacles you face. Let go of the difficulties that appear on your road. It is not up to you to worry about the "how it will happen" part of your journey. Just have faith that it *will* happen. Keep your goal always in the forefront of your mind.

Remember that belief in limitation is the one and only thing that causes limitation. The way you think is the key. Energy, power, everything influential in your life is available for you to call on through your positive thought. Rehearse being rich in your own mind. Envision driving the car you have always wanted, living in your dream home, well-dressed, surrounded by all the things that make life incredible for you. See it all in your mind's eye. Believe it to be true in this moment. Know that it is on the way to you right now. This kind of visioning is the first step in making all your dreams come true.

See the things you want as already yours, already in your possession. Expect that they are on their way to you. Think of them as YOURS, as already belonging to you.

Use your Imagination to develop your ideas, your Intuition to seek out others who are like-minded who will support you as you develop them, your Perception to understand what the steps are and what steps need to be taken next to advance your goals, your Will to keep yourself on track free from distractions and destruction, your Memory to help you recall the greatness in your life so far and your Reason to double-check and make sure that the choices you are making are ALWAYS moving you closer to your goal on your way to becoming a GPS Millionaire.

2. Our Natural Resources

The earth is abundant with natural resources that can help us towards our destination. Have you considered how that abundance can benefit your plans for Growth, Prosperity and

Success? Energy and Matter are the two substances of the Universe.

Take the time to determine what elements provided freely and abundantly in nature can support you in achieving your GPS Millionaire goals. You have far more available at your disposal from the world's bountiful natural resources than you have ever utilized or considered applying towards your life purpose to serve and support others.

With energy, you must learn to let it flow. People often say, "I have no energy." This is not true. You have an incredible amount of energy inside your body. You must learn to relax and let it flow so that you can receive more energy. That is how energy works. Energy dries up when you try to control it – the first thing you lose is its ability to flow freely. This blocking or hardening of energy is truly getting in your own way.

If you look at electricity, for example: it must be used. You cannot store electricity in massive quantities without prohibitively large expense. You can decide that you are not going to do anything for the next three days because on the fourth day you are going to take ALL the energy you have saved and use it to run a marathon. That kind of thinking simply won't work because there are MANY other factors that go into running a marathon race and you simply cannot save your energy in that way. Energy cannot be saved. It must be intelligently and effectively directed (i.e. used). Who is in charge of that? You are!

This is the beautiful thing about electricity – no one really knows exactly what it is. We all know how to use it, but where did it come from? It is described in many dictionaries as a physical phenomenon. Everyone has an idea about what causes electricity (charged electrons and protons), but no one seems to know how it originated or why it happens at all! This is not dissimilar from the metaphor of your car: you get in, you turn on the engine, and it works and off you go. Do you know how or why your car works? Most people don't. They just want to know that it works. The same is true of electricity, and we know MUCH less about it than we know about our car.

There is MUCH to learn from observing electricity. It FLOWS in a CURRENT and it can do so in LARGE quantities in POSITIVE and NEGATIVE charges! Study electricity with the mindset to consider ways that you can apply the principle of FLOW in your life to stay in a CURRENT taking you in a LARGE stream towards your POSITIVE result of becoming a GPS Millionaire! That is the way to apply the principles of electricity into YOUR life. You will KNOW that you have become electrified when things start to happen for you.

Similarly, you know that this thinking can also take you very quickly in the WRONG direction with a NEGATIVE impulse. Think of a massive hydro station that goes on overload. What is the result? Overload and widespread BLACKOUT! Don't ever go there! Stay POSITIVE and realize that the secret to maintaining a healthy FLOW is to ALWAYS consider whether you are moving CLOSER TO or FURTHER AWAY from what you want. Measure your results and think! Use your inner GPS to guide you to your desired destination. I KNOW you can do it if you apply this massive Gain Positive Solution.

3. GPS MindStorming

We all possess innate abilities that are very distinct from our logical or reasoning skills. It seems that human beings are born with many creative abilities – but sometimes our paradigms and our education cancel these out or we feel we are not strong enough to use our creative imaginations in a positive and supporting way in our lives. We fail to connect or recognize the creative patterns that can help us move forward to achieve success in our projects. That is because your creative ideas are similar to your muscles – if you do not exercise them, they lose their strength and even wither away because of lack of use. There is a way for you to access this creativity and have a lot of fun along the way.

There is a simple way to begin to exercise your creativity today. Get your favorite comfort beverage (coffee, tea, juice or water will do!) and a sheet of paper. What you want to do is get in a space where you can work on your own in an uninterrupted way for about 30-60 minutes or so. First, you must frame your issue in one or two words and write them inside a circle in the center of the piece of paper.

I want you to look at and consider the following GPS MindMap and look at it closely:

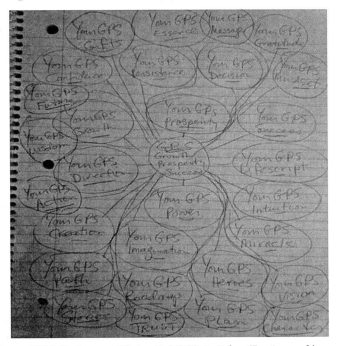

Example – GPS Mindmap of Potential GPS Articles, Topics and/or Audio/Video Blogs

In this example you can see the results of my personal efforts to develop and expand the GPS Brand with my ideas for potential Growth, Prosperity and Success (GPS) articles, topics and audio/video blogs. This was created by me in August, 2015 and I am sharing it with you so that you can see the profound impact you can have on your own growth.

I decided to identify the solutions and answers for a couple of problems or issues that I wanted resolved as quickly as possible by getting quiet and relaxed so that I could devote the time to allowing important messages to come through to me. I went to my favorite quiet coffee shop, sat with my coffee and my sheet of paper UNINTERRUPTED for 30-60 minutes and generated this sheet in one sitting. I was amazed and thrilled with the results which have formed the basis for my proceeding to develop my business through this process. I have developed other similar mindmaps with this incredible process.

It is a process you can learn and grow from as well. Simply identify areas where you are definitely in need of help to develop solutions for the future. It can be anything, whether in your personal or professional life. Then, find a quiet space for 30-60 minutes with a blank sheet of paper and a beverage of your choice and begin. Place the problem you are seeking to solve in 1-2 words in a circle in the center of the paper. Begin writing down immediately whatever comes into your mind as potential solutions. Write it down in 1-2 words so you can remember it, and enclose it in a circle and connect it with a line to you central problem. Do NOT judge or assess what you come up with. Do NOT say "That won't work!" – Just accept for now that it will! In the process of GPS MindStorming you must focus on your thoughts, stay open, and simply write down what comes up. There will be time for you to assess, then accept or reject or prioritize what you have written down later.

This simple process of creatively addressing your thinking and recording the words that emerge for a problem you have identified can transform your thinking to a much better place in your world as you take action on the ideas you generate in the near future. It is a mind-boggling, 'piece of gold' process that can take your life on a Growth, Prosperity and Success journey straight to your GPS Millionaire!

Be a person of INCREASE. Always bring more value to the table than you take away and your results will skyrocket. This is a metaphor for INCREASE. Use your creative imagination in this new way and your results will GROW in an exponential manner. You can expand your thinking and add more value by using the GPS MindStorming technique to create more abundance in your life based on your great ideas, abilities and unique talents....and this is a practical way to develop those ideas!! Your goal with this new approach is to create ways to

GROW your income every month and add VALUE to your business, instead of the other way around!

Here is the truth – you must change your old programming to see how you can move forward to achieve exponential growth on your way to becoming a GPS Millionaire! If nothing else in this book has convinced you of that, this example of a new way of thinking should have you CONVINCED that you now understand what you need to do to become a GPS Millionaire.

Change your thinking! Break those old paradigms that have held you in their grip for years! Many people still do not get that they are chained by their old thinking. You do! *You* are on your way to becoming a GPS Millionaire because *you* have learned about it and are taking ACTION on it! Use GPS MindStorming for yourself on your projects and ideas - that is the kind of thinking that will move you creatively, imaginatively into your new GPS World of Wealth!

4. Charting Your Life!

We all want our lives to be better; most of us do NOT want to consider ourselves 'statistics.' We feel de-personalized, de-humanized, reduced. How can statistics possibly help us to increase who we are and where we want to go? As a result of this kind of thinking, we dismiss ANY attempts anyone else makes to classify us as statistics. We just can't seem to bear the thought of it.

It is like aging – we don't want to consider it, we want to remain eternally young and youthful. So we do all kinds of crazy things to prevent it from happening, although logically we know that the aging of our bodies is a process. Truly, it is just a process that we must learn to face directly. There is a lot we can do with our mindset and our attitude to make the process of aging enjoyable. I am looking forward to it, because I know that with each passing day I am getting better and better! ...and so are YOU!

The truth is that your sub-conscious mind does not age! That is great news! In fact, your sub-conscious mind does not classify time and space. You know this to be true because when you are fully involved with something you are PASSIONATE about and that you LOVE doing time and space floats well beyond your awareness. What happens? You look at your watch and say, "Where did the time go? We've been here for hours and it only felt like 15 minutes had gone by!!"

Where *does* the time go? It doesn't go anywhere – it didn't exist because you were fully engaged with your sub-conscious mind doing amazing, loving and passionate things that you care deeply about! You may have even lost touch with where you were when that happened – it doesn't matter to you at that time. What matters is the primacy of that passionate experience! You will go to a movie theater with a large group of total strangers and find yourself, when you are enthused about the movie, transported into a space somewhere far away from that theater and those total strangers. How does that happen? You are still in that same cold, popcorn-smelling theater with those unknown strangers in the dark!! It is the power of your subconscious mind in action!

But, for our purposes in this chapter, we want to call you back to your rational, reasoning mind. You still inhabit that physical body of yours while these experiences are occurring. You need to have a reference point that will allow you to see exactly WHERE you are in your life spectrum on the chart of aging. More importantly, what remains, what potential, approximate time on this planet do you have left available for you to achieve, contribute and give back in the world all of the unique gifts, talents, and abilities you have to make a difference to better this world? How can you pursue your Growth, Prosperity and Success in your journey to become a GPS Millionaire with the very best information available to make the wise decisions required to keep you on course to your goal?

If you want to turn the impossible into the possible you have to apply your energy. Each of us comes to this planet with a limited amount of total life energy. The portion you have been given is actually equal to your Total Life Energy. Every moment we spend is time that we trade for our Total Life Energy.

Study the numbers on this chart to determine your approximate position:

Total Life Energy Remaining:

Age	Years	Days	Hours
20	56.3	20,540	493,525
25	51.6	18,835	452,325
30	46.9	17,118	411,125
35	42.2	15,403	369,925
40	37.6	13,725	329,600
45	33.0	12,045	289,275
50	28.6	16,439	250,710
55	24.4	8,906	213,890
60	20.5	7,484	179,705
65	16.9	6,168	148,145
70	13.6	4,964	119,218
75	10.7	3,905	98,796

Have you ever looked at your life in this way? Probably not. We are unique and precious beings and it is painful to consider that there is an end in sight for us in our physical body as we know it. Most of us do not want to consider the transition that we ALL must face at some point. Why is that? Because it is TOO PAINFUL for many of us. This chart offers a GAIN and PAIN snapshot of our lives at the same time. A GPS Millionaire looks into the future without fear and considers everything to INCREASE their awareness and contribution to others! This is my gift to your awareness – use it to your advantage immediately for your future and don't look back for a moment! How will you use this information to better the world and to expand your contribution and service? With the time that remains for you – Focus your mind in one direction to be effective. Remember your goal: keep it positive!

Congratulations! You are on your way to becoming a GPS Millionaire!

5. Join The GPS Club!

As you are moving forward with your life in a positive manner, your world can still be surrounded heavily by negative and destructive influences that restrain you and try their best to knock you off course. These forces are in your life and around your life because of the way you have thought in the past to this point. The receptors or satellites from The GPS Mind Mapper remind us that we too often react to the outside world and get knocked off course. You can change this in your life! It sounds silly but – in order to change your life, you have to change your life!

When you see merit and value in new information, you must make a positive decision to choose to use that information to move your life to a better place. You may be currently in a work situation that is holding you back, you may have friends that have been dragging you down with their negativity, you may have had family members, or even a partner, who have 'rained on your parade' with negative vibes when you got enthusiastic and excited about pursuing something positive in your life.

Here is the good news. You don't need their approval. What they think is actually none of your business. They are allowed to be who they are. They are just NOT allowed and do NOT have permission to tell you what to think or do – STOP giving away your life power.

You may want to evaluate your life – career, friends, family, and relationships – and make some decisions how you need to change what is going on. This may involve considering other career options, getting some new friends, avoiding contact with certain negative family members to even considering whether you are in a relationship with a good future. I am not referring here to the "what have you done for me lately" syndrome. I am speaking about the energy and attitude that comes with your current relationships – from friends, co-workers, family and your partner. Make a decision quietly inside to have them go in the best possible direction for your Growth, Prosperity and Success or you will not tolerate being in them. You want to ensure that you are accessing the best possible energy for you in order to achieve your GPS Millionaire. You deserve it! You deserve the best because--You're the Best! YTB!

Part of your plan is to be among people who share that same passion and energy to move your life forward. Who is that? Well, it can take many possible faces; however, one tremendous face is that of the Mastermind. What is a Mastermind? It is usually a group of people committed to helping each other be the best that they can be. To be open to learning and suggestions from like-minded people who can offer you their best advice on how you can best move forward in your life. You also contribute to this group by offering your insights on their commitment to their own lives and how they can best move forward to achieve their goals. You share your insights and experience for their benefit, while receiving their insights and experiences to benefit you!! It is a HUGE win-win situation.

That is the goal of The GPS Club. To enable like-minded participants world-wide to Mastermind together to help each other achieve their dreams using the principles of the GPS Millionaire and The Secret of the Ages for the 21st Century! WOW! What an unbeatable combination.

Go to www.thegpsclub.com to sign up and watch as your life continues toward Growth, Prosperity and Success as you develop and help friends around the globe in your online meetings as we have and continue to do!

You need to go back and re-read this chapter several times. It contains HUGE information that you need to take action on right away. Re-read it with a spirit of new openness to your unique potential and ability to make these ideas your own and to apply them via your imaginative and creative mind in order to achieve your goals. This material MUST be applied – merely chatting about it, reflecting on it, or rejecting it and putting it down will in no way help you at all!

You are here. It is now and we know it. If you are NOT going to ACT on this material in your life – when will you? The last time I looked 'someday' was NOT a day in the week. Use your life energy in a positive, effective and productive way to change what you are doing. Become a member of The GPS Club and position yourself on the road towards your GPS Millionaire. Take these Gain or Pain Solutions and go for the GAIN! You will NEVER regret what you will learn, how much better your life will be, and the new person you will become. Make the decision now and GO FOR IT!! YTB!! Join with us and be the next GPS Millionaire!

Your mind is part and parcel of Universal Mind. You have the wisdom of all the ages to draw upon. Use it! Use it to do your work in a way it was never done before. Use it to find new outlets for your business, new methods of reaching people, new and better ways of serving them. Use it to uncover new riches, to learn ways to make the world a better place to live in.

Robert Collier

Chapter Seventeen

Give Profound Service

For the Law of Attraction is service. We receive in proportion as we give out. In fact, we usually receive in far greater proportion...It pays to give a little more value than seems necessary, to work a bit harder than you are paid for. It's that extra ounce of value that counts...It matters not how small your service – using it will make it greater...In other words, if you would be great, you must serve. And he who serves most shall be greatest of all.

Robert Collier

Life is NOT about getting, it is about giving. We have been raised to believe that there is a "pie" out there and we must work our butts off to get our "slice" of it, and that it will be big or small depending on how "hard" we work for it. What we never realized or weren't told were the negative ideas behind this thinking. First off, that the pie is a finite size – it can't be any bigger than that, and we must struggle, fight, and claw for only a small portion of it. This is also where the idea of losing is born – if we don't get our slice, we lose. We are called losers. Do you see how negative this is? Well, you might say that there have to be winners and losers. This type of thinking ensures that there will be MANY more losers than there are winners in life.

This is NOT the GPS Millionaire way.

It's time to recognize that we are not discussing widgets here – each "slice" represents a person in this model. A person is a soul – *you* are a soul. A soul is timeless and has no time or space. It was mentioned previously that when you are doing something that you love time just seems to fly by – you are completely unaware of time's passing. That is because your soul, your higher self, your sub-conscious mind does not care that much about time and space. Certainly it is aware. However, if you close your eyes and put away your birth certificate for a moment – How old does your soul think you are? Does it really care how old you are? I don't think it does – but definitely your ego does. We must begin to become aware of this tremendous gift we possess in our marvelous mind. It can help us to rise above what seems to be happening in our lives to see the truth in front of us. Things are NOT what they seem; no matter how bad, or how good, they may appear. This is the solution (and the problem) to EVERYTHING in our lives.

Many fortunes can begin when individuals (employees) see customer needs that are not being met and that their current employer has no interest in satisfying those specific needs. This can often be the case because businesses are sometimes not focused to grow their results from responding to customer inquiries or complaints to create more business. The individual employee decides that he or she will start a new business, sometimes on the side, to meet the needs of these customers and give them what they are really asking for that their current employer is missing. That can be all that is needed to move you on your journey to your GPS Millionaire.

To grow your own business, look for something that is an improvement on an existing product or service rather than something brand new. Look for something that is cheaper or of better quality or a niche in the marketplace that is not being well served. Look for something that has additional features or functions that current products or services don't offer. Look for something that is an improvement in some way on something that people are already buying and using.

Improving an existing successful product or service is the fastest and surest way to build a successful business. An idea only needs to be a little bit newer and better to capture substantial market share.

Look for something that represents genuine value. Seek a product or service that makes an important contribution to the quality of life or work of the customer. Don't look for easy money. Don't look for gimmicks or get-rich-quick schemes or rewards without working. There aren't any. Always strive to Give Profound Service to the marketplace and to your customers and your GPS will flow back to you.

We also need to understand that when we Give Profound Service lives are changed – often enough from charitable giving. But it shouldn't end there. When we begin to recognize that each person we deal with in our lives is a soul, then we are in a position to see the fantastic strength inside each person. We are all different, yet we are all the same, as you learned in an earlier chapter with The GPS Mind Mapper. People can demonstrate, whether wealthy or not, that they are giving, loving and caring by the kindnesses they share with others. People can give their time, their money, their talents, their abilities, their passions to thousands of different life-enhancing endeavors on a daily basis and make a real difference in our world.

The giving does not have to be public or done in order to receive credit and recognition. Often the best giving is done when no one knows that you have given anything, perhaps even the recipient does not know that you gave them the gift. This is true giving of the highest kind. Giving publicly, where everyone takes note of what you gave and how much, is really more show for others, than true giving. You must give freely and from the heart with no expectation of return.

My friend, Bob Proctor, gives selflessly to many. He loves to give to help build schools in Africa by supporting his friend, Cynthia Kersey, who started the Unstoppable Foundation – they are a most worthy organization doing amazing work that deserves great support- http://unstoppablefoundation.org

For six years I served on the Board of Directors of Delisle Youth Services in Toronto, ON – a social service agency dedicated to helping youth and their families. As a High School principal, I watched, often helplessly, as children with difficult physical, mental health and family issues struggled to function as 'normal' students in school. I realized that they were often marginalized by the system and eventually forced to leave because they were unable, for various health and personal reasons, to cope with the daily regimen of attending classes at the high school level and their studying responsibilities, while trying to cope with enormous personal issues in their young lives. These were mostly brave and courageous teen individuals who certainly did NOT deserve to be treated as "bad students." Yet that is often how the education system and teachers perceived them, without giving it a thought. These kinds of students (people) being somehow less than the rest. This is a kind of Social Darwinism, a horribly self-serving and negative idea.

The school system being unable to help them, agencies like Delisle Youth Services in Toronto, ON rolled up their sleeves and DID help – in a big way. They listened to their concerns, got involved with their families and made a big difference in helping them to continue with their education with positive support outside the school setting in small classrooms at the agency with supportive teachers and counsellors. So, I became passionate about supporting that agency (and similar agencies that help children and families) and served for 6 years to give back to my community. This organization does amazing work in Toronto – check them out. http://delisleyouth.org

Giving back to others is a tremendous way to share your skills, talents and abilities. My experience has been that I receive far more from my giving than I ever expected in terms of new friends, experiences and opportunities. When you focus to Give Profound Service to others, your rewards are amplified and given back to you in ways that you never considered before. I recommend this process highly to everyone reading this book that is committed to taking action to become a GPS Millionaire!

People enjoy giving and develop abundance from sharing their own Growth, Prosperity and Success. You always get what you give – it comes back to you. We aren't necessarily aware of how that happens, but it does. Life is a circle and what you give to the world is returned to you, often amplified and expanded and you are duly rewarded through life's abundance. By giving to others you indirectly draw more to yourself. What you focus on expands! This enables and facilitates more giving and more receiving – it is a beautiful and continuous concept that can create outstanding flow and enrichment in your life and the lives of others. Try it! You will connect with your inner GPS and your life will be changed for the better.

When we look at other people and truly see them as individual souls, it becomes clear how each of them is 'hard-wired' with special gifts, talents and abilities. Every soul is piloted by their gifts! You can see it if you observe their behavior closely. Their passions are directing their lives. What gifts do you have inside? What gifts do you have that you are hiding or concealing to the world? What gifts do you need to grow and develop to make the world a better place? What contribution can you make with the gifts you possess to improve the lives of others? How can you share yourself and Give Profound Service to others?

When we Give Profound Service – we see every person in a very different way. We see everyone trying their best to be the best possible person they can be on this earth. We see people trying hard to make a difference in the lives of others, trying to make the world a better place for all of us. Because of this GPS you are enjoying, everything you put out into this world is a gift! That is a phenomenal idea, and it is a true fact!

Understand that the future belongs to those who continue learning, and as each of us seeks to apply our giving to what we are learning, we will be making ever and ever greater contributions to the advancement of LIFE! There can be no finer calling than helping others, our fellow souls, to be the best that they can be. This is the basis of the thought: if I can do it, you can do it.

Who have you mentored today? Who have you brought the message of a positive attitude to today? How have you made a difference in the lives of others? When you think about the many ways that you can Give Profound Service, your creativity and imagination kick in and you begin to generate ideas that can really help and make a difference in the lives of others.

How can I help? How can I serve others? These are great questions to ask as you offer to Give Profound Service.

What can you give that will help others? You may not think you have the ability to do that – but that is far from the truth. You possess so many gifts inside you that they cannot be recorded. To activate them, however, you have to take action to share them. You have to take your light out from under the table where you have been hiding it and let others see it and enjoy and marvel in it.

Yes, there will always be those who criticize you for what you are doing or trying to do. That must NOT stop you anymore. Do not listen to critical people who attempt to minimize or prevent what you wish to give to others. Make a decision that you are not going to be turned away by the opinions of others on this one. You are here, it is now, and you have a right to give everything to anything that you are passionate about. Just make a start to do it!

The greatest gift is a portion of thyself.
Ralph Waldo Emerson

It's really about going the extra mile, isn't it? Someone said that there are no traffic jams on the extra mile. This is very true. The top ten percent are the ones you will find there. The masses don't know about the extra mile – it is something foreign to their thinking. Many, many people choose not to be aware of it. But it is still there waiting for someone to come along and travel it – alone! It would NOT be a special place to be, if there were lots of people on it. By giving of yourself to others, you are giving a very precious and unique gift. You are to be commended and acknowledged for choosing to Give Profound Service.

Life is NOT a dress rehearsal – this is it, the time is now! Get started and begin to Give Profound Service in a way that demonstrates your connection with your inner GPS, your Higher Self. It is time for you to think, really THINK. Think of the concepts that you have studied in the preceding chapters – Great Purposes Support, Grander Personal Surprises, Giveaway Past Situations, Growth Principle – Gratitude, Growth Principle – Serenity, Growth Principle – Spirituality, Growth Principle – Success, Greater Potential Self, Generous Prosperity Sensibility, Goals Predict Success, Genius Power Stimulates, Great People Surround, Gain Profitable Synergy, Grow Powerful Self, Gain or Pain Solutions, Give Profound Service, Genuine Positive Sensitivity and Growth, Prosperity and Success. This is the GPS Millionaire System! Use it! Live it! Make your dreams a reality!

You have been provided with a GPS Wealth of information! Your inner GPS is waiting to take you on the journey to your GPS Millionaire life. It's an exciting and profound journey of change, an expanding of your mind to a new way of thinking. I know that when you look back a year from now, after you first take action on these ideas, you will see MASSIVE growth in yourself and you will always be grateful for having developed the wisdom to learn and do what is best for you. You know that these ideas will take you in the best direction because this is the BEST information you could possibly have to connect with your inner GPS (your Higher Self) and your growing awareness of all that life has to offer.

Follow this simple formula: Study, Think and Do – and your inner GPS will truly become Your Roadmap for Growth, Prosperity and Success.

Join us now, sign up for more GPS training and make it happen - and remember YTB! (You're the Best!)

The people to whom riches and abundance flow so easily are those who have widened their channels by looking for plenty, by expecting it and by preparing for it through continual and ever-increasing service.

Robert Collier

Chapter 18

Genuine Positive Sensitivity

Enjoy these GPS Millionaire Wisdom Cards that inspire and motivate – let the words on them infuse your spirit with a Genuine Positive Sensitivity that guides your inner GPS to take action continuously to improve YOU and what you are seeking to contribute to enhance and serve the lives of others!

**Dream bold Dreams
- and then live them!**
- Bob Proctor

> **Escape the sea of sameness!**
> — *Raymond Aaron*

> **Be the hero of your life, Not the Victim. It is your own belief in yourself that counts the most!**
> — *Bruce McGregor*

> **You have to harness and direct the power of your thoughts.**
> — *Jack Canfield*

> No matter how stupendous and complicated,
> nor how simple your problem may be –
> the solution of it lies within yourself.
> — Robert Collier

> Be bold enough to claim that
> it is your right to be rich and your
> deeper mind will honor your claim.
> — Dr. Joseph Murphy

> Focus on what you want!
> (instead of what you don't want.)
> — Dr. Robert Anthony

> Aspire to the attainment of inward nobility,
> not outward glory, and begin
> to attain it where you now are.
> — *James Allen*

> You are not a finished product —
> You are a work in progress!
> — *Bruce McGregor*

> What you are going to be —
> what success you will reach —
> is being decided by
> the action you are taking now.
> — *Robert Collier*

> Many of the things you can count,
> don't count.
> Many of the things you can't count,
> really count.
> — *Albert Einstein*

> To achieve the marvelous, it is precisely
> the unthinkable that must be thought.
> — *Tom Robbins*

> Obstacles are like wild animals. They are cowards but they will bluff you if they can. If they see you are afraid of them…they are liable to spring upon you, but if you look them squarely in the eye, they will slink, out of sight.
> — *Orison Swett Marden*

> No matter how many forces try to make you be like everyone else, the scientific truth is that in all of the earth's history there has never been another person exactly like you, and there never will be again.
> - Robert K. Cooper, PhD.

> Each man should frame life so that at some future hour fact and his dreaming meet.
> - Victor Hugo

> There are two basic forms of adapting as things change. One way is the brain's automatic reaction – trying harder, and tensing up leading to exhaustion. The other form of adaptation is the application of fluid intelligence to find new and even better ways to achieve your dreams.
> - Bruce McGregor

> **Since new developments are
> the products of a creative mind,
> we must therefore stimulate
> and encourage that type of mind
> in every way possible.**
> — *George Washington Carver*

> **One very important aspect of motivation
> is the willingness to stop and to look at things
> that no one else has bothered to look at.
> This simple process of focusing on things
> that are normally taken for granted
> is a powerful source of creativity.**
> — *Edward de Bono*

> **Those who dream by day are
> cognizant of many things
> which escape those who
> only dream by night.**
> — *Edgar Allan Poe*

> You've got to choose discipline,
> versus regret, because
> discipline weighs ounces
> and regret weighs tons.
> - Jim Rohn

> As a single footstep will not make a path
> on the earth, so a single thought
> will not make a pathway on the mind.
> To make a deep physical path,
> we walk again and again.
> To make a deep mental path,
> we must think over and over the kind of
> thoughts we wish to dominate our mind.
> - Henry David Thoreau

> Whatever you do, if you do it sincerely,
> will eventually become a bridge
> to your wholeness,
> a good ship that carries you
> through the darkness.
> - Dr. Carl Jung

> People are like stained-glass windows.
> They sparkle and shine when the sun is out,
> but when the darkness sets in,
> their true beauty is revealed
> only if there is a light from within.
> — Elisabeth Kubler-Ross

> Strengths are like gold
> - you've got to get them out of
> the ground before you can use them.
> — Brian Tracy

> The truth is that we react to the vision we create
> and hold – and so do all the cells in our body.
> So it's vitally important to hold a clear vision
> of ourselves as deserving of feeling inspired,
> knowing that it's our ultimate calling and
> choosing to be in-Spirit
> even when everything around us
> suggests otherwise.
> — Dr. Wayne Dyer

> Keep away from people who try to belittle
> your ambitions. Small people always do that,
> but the really great make you feel
> that you, too, can become great.
> - *Mark Twain*

> The grateful mind is constantly fixed
> upon the best.
> Therefore it tends to become the best.
> It takes the form or character of the best,
> and will receive the best.
> - *Wallace D. Wattles*

> Be thankful for what you have; you'll end up
> having more. If you concentrate on what you
> don't have, you'll never, ever have enough.
> - *Oprah Winfrey*

> Think of yourself as on the threshold
> of unparalleled success.
> A whole, clear, glorious life lies before you.
> Achieve! Achieve!
> — *Andrew Carnegie*

> We ought, so far as it lies within our power,
> to aspire to immortality, and do all that
> we can to live in conformity with the highest
> that is within us; for even if it is small in
> quantity, in power & preciousness,
> it far excels all the rest.
> — *Aristotle*

> It is only the ignorant
> who despise education.
> — *Pubilius Syrus*
> (85-43 BC)

About Bruce McGregor

Bruce McGregor is an Award Winning Author and a Mentor and Speaker from Toronto, Canada.

Bruce is a former High School Principal who served nearly 35 years in public education in Canada. He has degrees from the University of Toronto and Queen's University and holds qualifications with Ontario's Ministry of Education as a Principal and a Superintendent. Bruce also had experience working in the automobile parts industry, for the Toronto Transit Commission, as a professional musician, musical director and symphony orchestra conductor, Musician-In-Residence at Trent University, Visiting Assistant Professor at the University of Toronto, as a high school teacher, education consultant, administrator, Vice-Principal and Principal. In addition, he has worked as a consultant, real estate property manager, author and success mentor and started his own business a few years ago – McGregor & Associates Services, in Toronto. Bruce now does business with his friends and colleagues around the world.

Bruce began studying and researching inspiring personal growth materials on a daily basis and began to see his life changing each and every day. When the time came to decide whether to continue his very successful career as a Principal in one of Canada's finest public high schools, Bruce decided eagerly, after serving literally thousands of parents, students & teachers that he had other exciting roads to travel.

From 2008-2016, Bruce took action on these principles, along with his wife Gail, to support and grow the value of family-held rental real estate by hundreds of thousands of dollars, while generating a healthy income and very positive cash flow. In 2012, Bruce was responsible for preparing and selling family properties, including his own home, generating a tax-free profit of over $1.5 million with no capital gains. This result created a completely mortgage-free lifestyle for Bruce & his family.

Bruce has been fortunate to be mentored by Raymond Aaron New York Times Top Ten Best Selling Author, Mentor and World-Renowned Speaker and friend. Bruce has also worked extensively with Bob Proctor and considers him to be an amazing & wonderful friend and with Peggy McColl, New York Times Best Selling Author, also an amazing mentor and friend.

Bruce McGregor's goal with the *GPS Millionaire* book is to provide you with easy access to these ideas and concepts, and to renew and update the work of Robert Collier for the 21st Century. Bruce now devotes his creative imagination and ability to developing and sharing these ideas with you into the future to enable and empower you to live and prosper in a way that enhances your lifestyle and supports you & your family in achieving your goals in life!